DRAGONS, WITCHES,
AND OTHER FANTASY CREATURES IN
ORIGAMI

Mario Adrados Netto
and J. Aníbal Voyer Iniesta

DOVER PUBLICATIONS, INC.
Mineola, New York

Bibliographical Note

This Dover edition, first published in 2005, is a new English translation of
Seres de Ficción—El Lado Oscuro de la Papiroflexia, originally published in
Spanish by Editorial Miguel A. Salvatella, S.A., Barcelona, Spain, in 2000, and
includes all of the original diagrams and illustrations. The text of Part 5 from the
original Spanish edition has been omitted here, but all of the diagrams for con-
structing the wasp figure have been retained.

Library of Congress Cataloging-in-Publication Data

Netto, Mario Adrados.
    [Seres de ficción-el lado oscuro de la papiroflexia. English]
    Dragons, witches, and other fantasy creatures in origami / Mario Adrados
Netto, J. Aníbal Voyer Iniesta.
        p. cm.
    ISBN-13: 978-0-486-44212-9 (pbk.)
    ISBN-10: 0-486-44212-8 (pbk.)
    1. Origami. 2. Dragons in art. 3. Witches in art. 4. Animals, Mythical, in
art. I. Iniesta J. Aníbal Voyer. II. Title.

TT870.N465 2005
736'.982—dc22

                                                            2005043292

Manufactured in the United States by Courier Corporation
44212804
www.doverpublications.com

Preface

According to the dictionary of the Real Spanish Academy, *paper folding* is the ability and art to transform a piece of paper by folding it conveniently, thereby creating figures of determinative creatures or objects.

If we look in the database of the Spanish Agency of the ISBN for this entry or "origami," which is the name of this art in Japanese, we would discover that between 1980 and 1999, there have been more than sixty different books published in Spain with the main subject of paper folding. Since almost all of these books are intended for beginners, most of their pages are dedicated to very simple figures, which allow the novice to understand the skills needed in paper folding, and the last pages of these books are devoted to more complex models.

Just like these other books, the first part of our book also concentrates on the beginning of origami, but it is quite different from most of the others, since this is not a book for beginners. Almost all of its pages are filled with figures of a high level of difficulty; therefore it is geared for a person who has some previous knowledge of this type of art.

Our work is an unusual book on paper folding, in that it concentrates on fantastic or mythological creatures. It is not the first one of its kind to have been published, but we believe it is the first written in Spain.

If you are interested in basic books on paper folding, this publishing company has a fantastic large collection for the apprenticeship, but if you have some previous knowledge and you want to extend it, this is the book for you.

About the Authors

My name is Mario Adrados Netto, I am 29 years old, and I have worked in various professions: printing service, clinic assistant, layoff coach, and now I work in a C & A store in Vaguada, Spain.

Ever since I was a little boy, I loved being creative; I was the inventor of my class. I still have various simple figures from my childhood. Later on I had to start working and forgot all about it, but one day, at 20 years old, someone showed me how to create a bird with flapping wings, and of course, I loved it. I bought some books and I discovered again all those delightful moments when I used to fold papers into figures.

5

Thanks to a newspaper ad, a couple of years later I went to an exposition where I met Julián González and Aníbal Voyer. Along with them, I got into the Spanish Association of Paper Folding, where I was now in contact with others who were crazy about paper folding. This association helped me develop my abilities in folding papers into figures as well as in making up new figures. Aníbal and I soon realized that we shared a passion for these fantastic figures. At the same time that our friendship was growing, our repertoire was also developing. Then it came to our minds that we had to do something with these creations. Aníbal was the one with the idea of creating a book about it. We had many different figures, but because we were so strict with the quality of the figures, we rejected many others. The result is this book, which, with a lot of work and care, we present to whomever wishes to enjoy it.

My name is José Aníbal Voyer Iniesta, my friends call me Aníbal. I was born in Jaén on March 17, 1970, and I am a technical engineer of public services. I knew paper folding since my childhood, because my father is a fanatic and he is always creating and folding new images and figures. However, it was not until I was 11 years old that this fanaticism grew in me.

My first contact with the association was peculiar in a way. Years ago, in a cafeteria, my father left an elephant figure guarding the tip on the table. By chance, Julián González saw the figure and left a business card for him so that he could contact him at the Spanish Association of Paper Folding. He did not seem that interested and he gave the card to me, but during that time I did not want to get involved.

In 1989 my sister saw in a window of a newspaper shop a collection of paper figures and decided to ask the owner to exchange a dragon (my first figure) for a killer whale. The owner accepted the exchange and she put me in contact with another member of the Spanish Association of Paper Folding, Juan Gimeno, who encouraged me tremendously. The next year, my creations occupied most of the places in my house.

It was around that time that I first met Mario. I was an instructor of paper folding in a cultural center with approximately twenty children. I was trying to explain to them, with little success, some traditional figures. It was then that Mario showed up, and helped me finish the class. Since then, our friendship has grown and I have never gone back to teaching kids.

In 1996 I participated, with not much expectation, in the 10th World Origami Exhibition, which was celebrated by NOA (Japanese Origami Association), and to my surprise, I won! As a reward I was invited to an origami convention in Kawabuchiko, at the bottom of the Fuji Mountains. This gave me an international reputation and since then, I have been invited to many more conventions.

Currently, my figures are in the hundreds and the general opinion is that they are not bad at all.

Introduction

For a long time I have enjoyed the world of fantasy, such as *The Lord of the Rings, Dragonlance,* etc. When I met Aníbal, we observed that our tastes were similar, not only because we read the same books, but because we could recreate them, thanks to paper folding.

We must say that from the start Aníbal held a certain advantage, since he already had several figures created, while I had barely begun and those figures seemed impossible to fold. Fortunately, I didn't despair and today I can show the figures that we have worked on.

Although some of the figures in this book appear to be very complicated, in reality you only need a bit of practice in following the instructions and folding. To make learning easier to those just beginning in the art of paper folding, we have included in the beginning of the book a few simple figures which do not devalue in the least the rest. These simpler figures permit you to learn the tricks of folding, and discover the pleasure of seeing how these figures, which at first may seem nearly impossible to construct, just appear within your fingers.

If you are beginning in paper folding, you will see that there are moments in which you will think it impossible to follow the instructions that appear in the book. Don't despair; little by little, what you have in your hands will soon take form. If you saw my first "works of art" and the faces on my friends and family when I'd show them, you would laugh.

My problem is that I was—and still am—quite anxious when folding and that drove me to be less meticulous than I should have been when starting a new figure. The first steps are the most important! Fold carefully at the start, and surely you will end better.

With this we arrive at another important point: the creation. Perhaps by the time you finish the book, it will seem impossible to invent anything new, but that's just not so. From each of the bases, intermediate steps, and even final steps, new and interesting possibilities can occur to you. If you get an inspiration along the lines of: "This reminds me of . . . ," I advise you to close the book—it won't move from there—and follow your muse where it takes you. Perhaps it won't come out exactly as you expected, but you will have taken a decisive step. You will have begun to create! Within each figure are many more that wish to be discovered by you.

If you are already familiar with paper folding, I expect that you will enjoy our figures. I hope that each one of them opens new possibilities for you, and that one day we should be the ones looking in the bookstore for one of *your* books.

MARIO ADRADOS NETTO

Index of Figures

Troll *(p. 18)*

Bat *(p. 20)*

Igor *(p. 22)*

Suit of Armor *(p. 24)*

Ghost *(p. 27)*

Sagittarius *(p. 29)*

Flying Serpent *(p. 34)*

Demon *(p. 37)*

Griffin *(p. 40)*

Cerberus *(p. 45)*

Wizard *(p. 49)*

Satyr *(p. 55)*

Unicorn *(p. 60)*

Sphinx *(p. 66)*

Centaur *(p. 73)*

Lady *(p. 82)*

Medusa *(p. 86)*

Mephistopheles *(p. 90)*

Pegasus *(p. 98)*

Oriental Dragon *(p. 108)*

Three-Headed Dragon *(p. 116)*

Dragon with Warrior *(p. 128)*

Dragon with Wizard *(p. 141)*

Witch *(p. 155)*

Wasp *(p. 167)*

Symbols

The symbols in paper folding are like words in a novel; if you don't understand them, the book is of little purpose to you. That is why it is very important that you familiarize yourself with their use and meaning, so that later you don't have problems folding the figures.

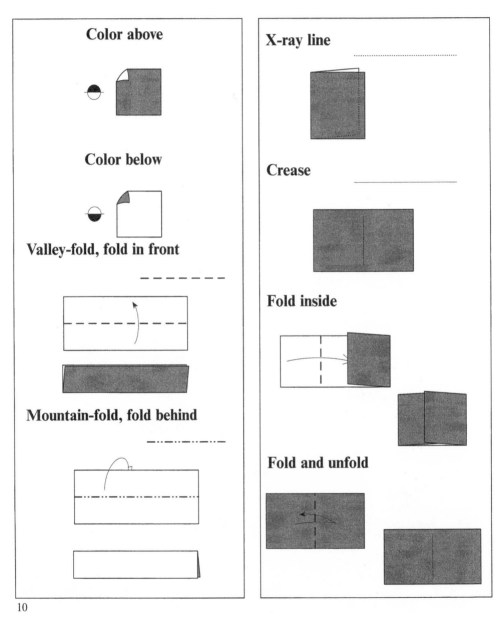

Color above

Color below

Valley-fold, fold in front

Mountain-fold, fold behind

X-ray line

Crease

Fold inside

Fold and unfold

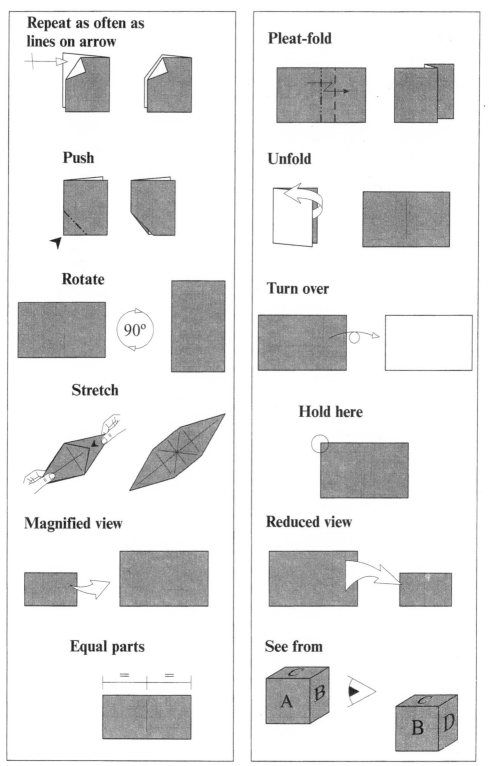

Repeat as often as lines on arrow

Push

Rotate

90°

Stretch

Magnified view

Equal parts

=   =

Pleat-fold

Unfold

Turn over

Hold here

Reduced view

See from

C

A   B

C

B   D

Bases

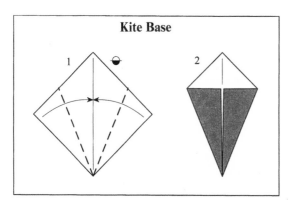

A base is a preliminary figure in which you can already appreciate the structure of angles and points of the finished model. There exists an infinite number of bases, on these pages you will find the more common ones.

(NOTE: The figures are only for decoration, they are not folded from these bases.)

Kite Base

Waterbomb Base

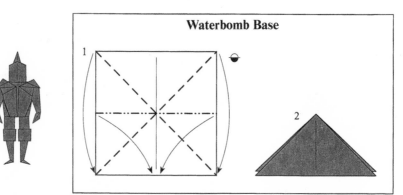

Preliminary Fold

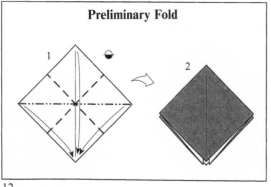

Fish Base

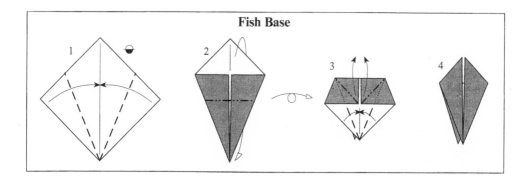

Bird Base

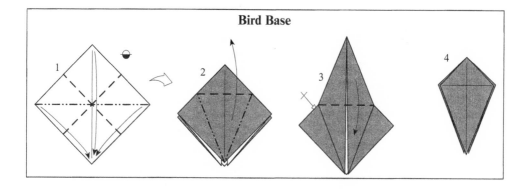

Frog Base

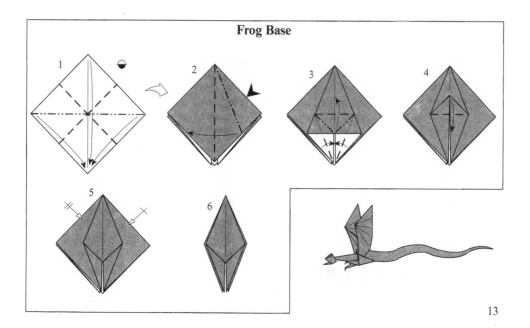

13

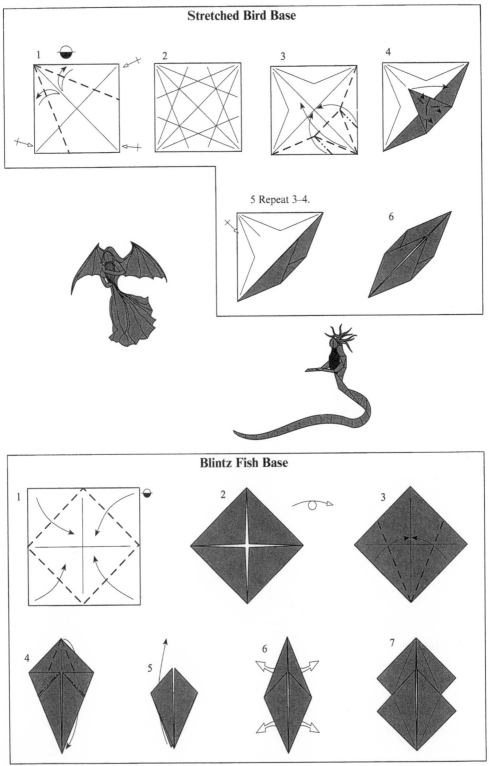

Stretched Bird Base

1

2

3

4

5 Repeat 3–4.

6

Blintz Fish Base

1

2

3

4

5

6

7

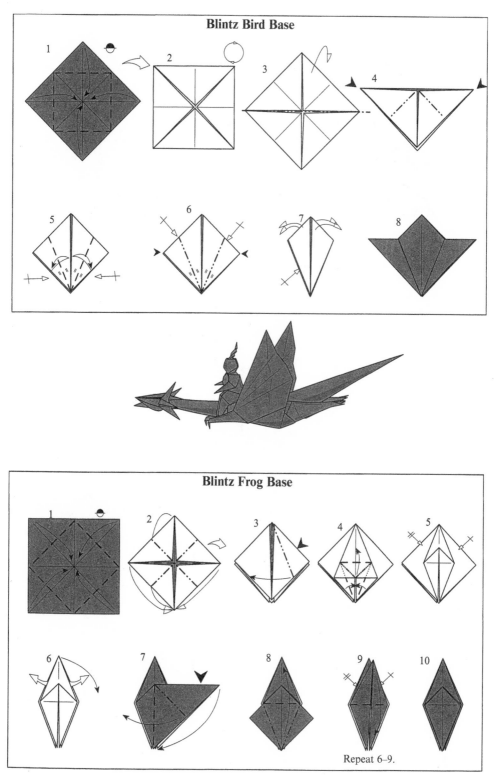

Blintz Bird Base

1

2

3

4

5

6

7

8

Blintz Frog Base

1

2

3

4

5

6

7

8

9

10

Repeat 6–9.

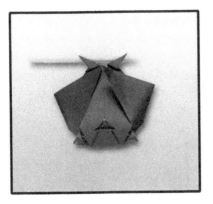

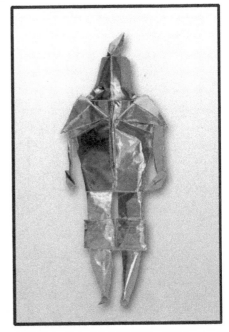

Part 1

Troll

Trolls are large beings with scaly skin and uncommon strength, controlled completely by evil. There are many reasons why they are on the dark side, including their hatred of the light, which burns them, and the sun, which turns them into stone.

Author: Mario Adrados Netto

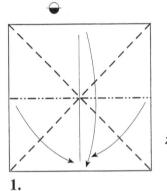

1.

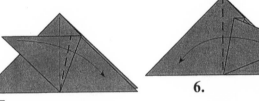

2.

3.

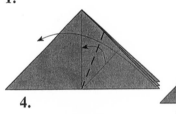

4.

5.

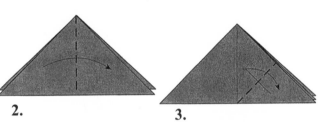

6.

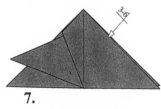

7.

8.

9.

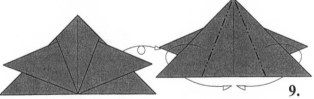

10.

11.

12.

18

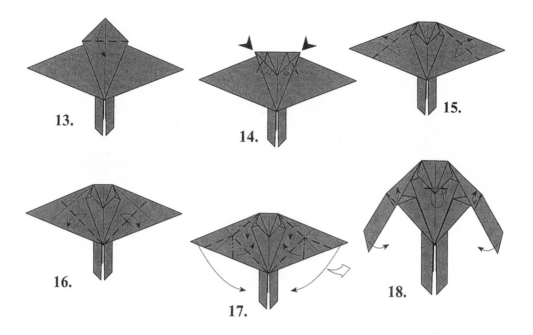

13.

14.

15.

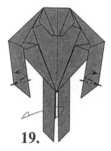

16.

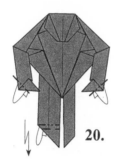

17.

18.

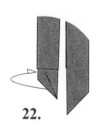

19.

20.

21.

22.

23.

19

Bat

Bats are mammals of the order Chiroptera. In heraldry they are represented frontally with their wings splayed. An ancient legend attributes the head of this mammal, after being well dried and suspended from the neck of a human, the power of not allowing sleep. It also symbolizes the vigilant, and awakes nature to foresee unfortunate accidents.

Author: Mario Adrados Netto

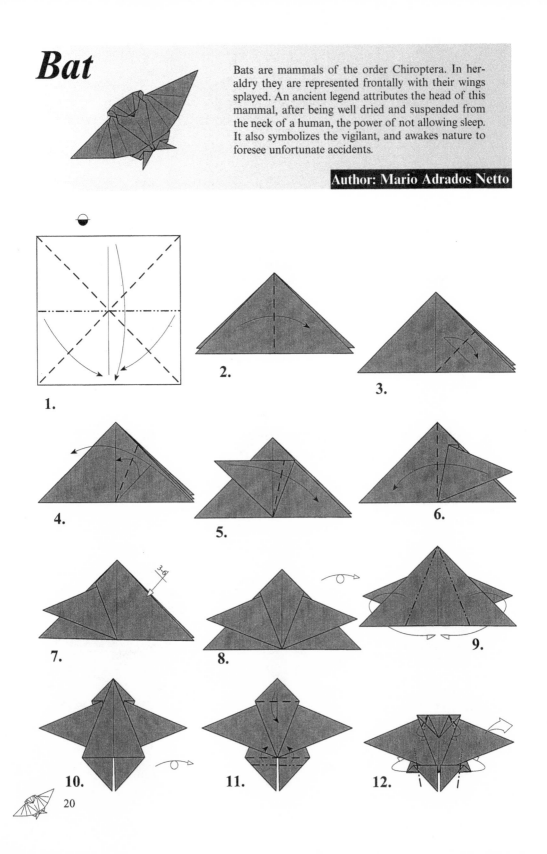

1.

2.

3.

4.

5.

6.

7.

8.

9.

10.

11.

12.

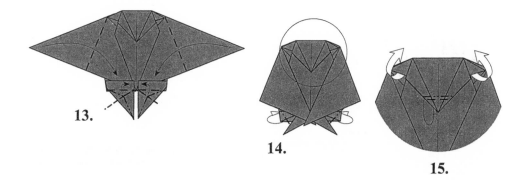

13.

14.

15.

16.

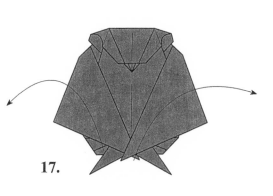

17.

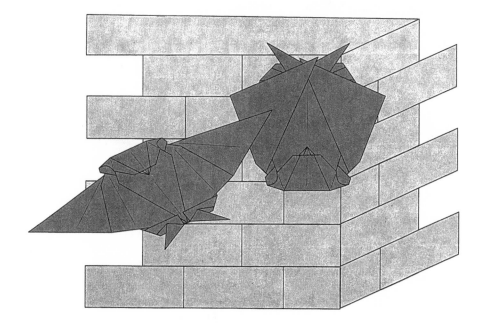

Igor

Igor was born to a humble family and his deformity made him grow up in absolute solitude. When Dr. Frankenstein offered him room, board, and a job, he knew that he would do anything for him. *Anything!*

Author: Mario Adrados Netto

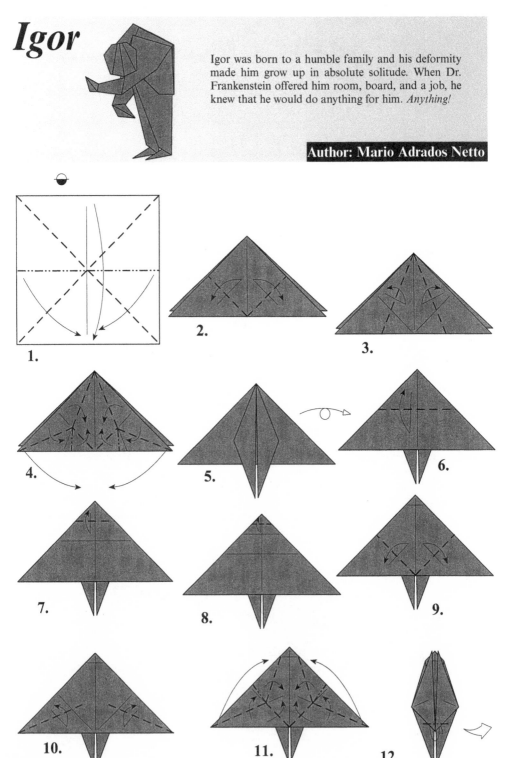

1.

2.

3.

4.

5.

6.

7.

8.

9.

10.

11.

12.

22

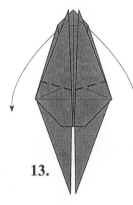

13.

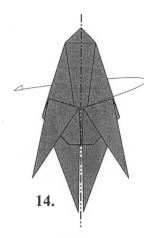

14.

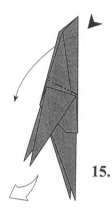

15.

16.

17.

18. Refold the head as you tuck the corner into the pocket.

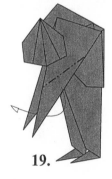

19.

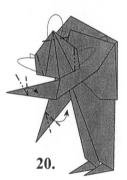

20.

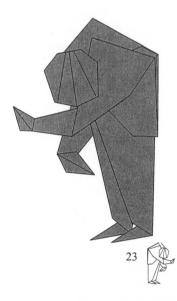

Suit of Armor

This is the union of pieces of steel that make up the defensive armor of the knights and men of war during the last period of the Middle Ages.

Author: Mario Adrados Netto

1.

2.

3.

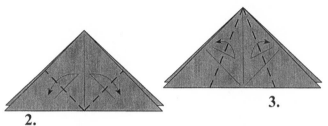

4.

5.

6.

7.

8.

9.

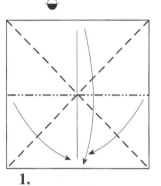

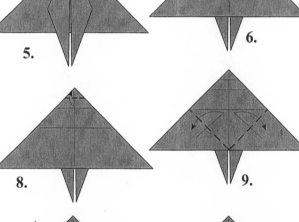

10.

11.

12.

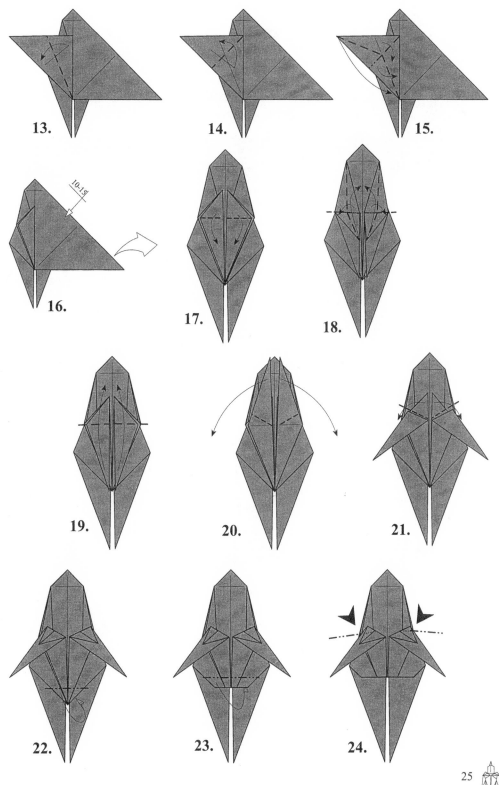

13.

14.

15.

16.

10-15°

17.

18.

19.

20.

21.

22.

23.

24.

25

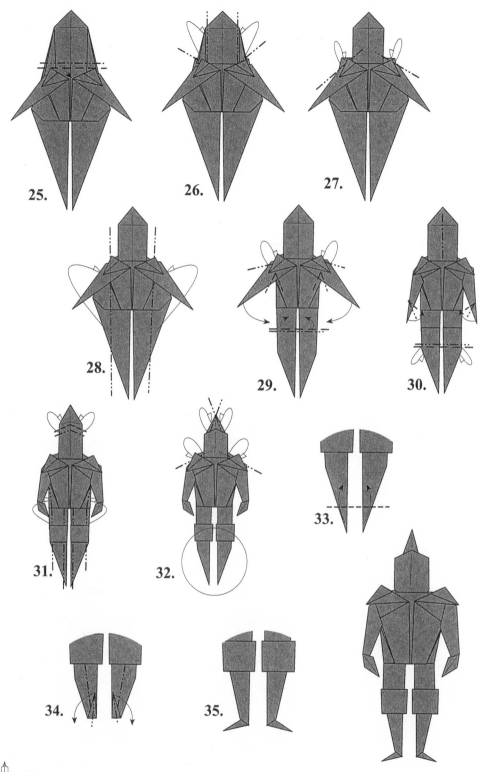

25.

26.

27.

28.

29.

30.

31.

32.

33.

34.

35.

Ghost

When a person dies dishonorably or is assassinated, his or her spirit is transformed into a phantom and stays condemned to wander the earth until it recovers its peace.

Authors: J. Aníbal - Francisco Voyer Iniesta

1.

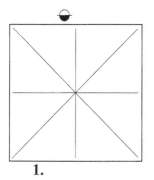
2.

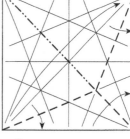
3.

4.

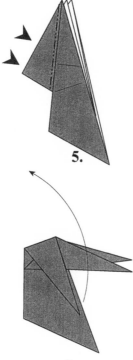
5.

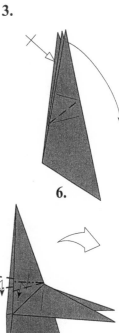
6.

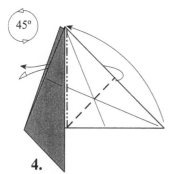
7.

8.

9.

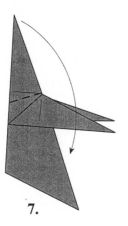

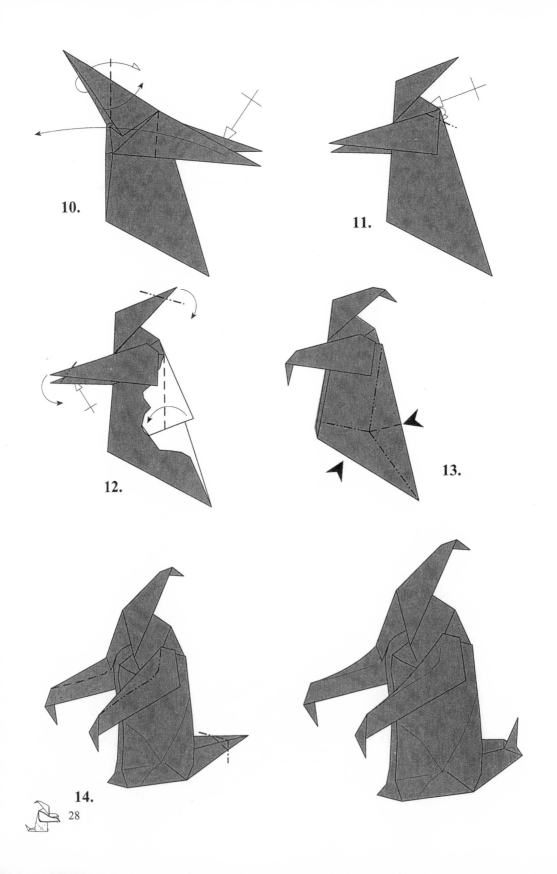

10.

11.

12.

13.

14.

28

Sagittarius

This chimerical figure is represented by a centaur, a beast that is half-man and half-horse. It is usually armed and ready with a bow and arrow.

Author: Mario Adrados Netto

1.

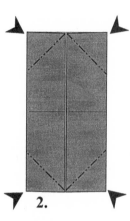

2.

3.

4.

5.

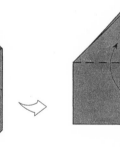

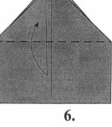

6.

7.

8.

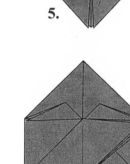

9.

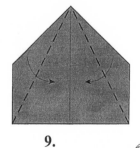

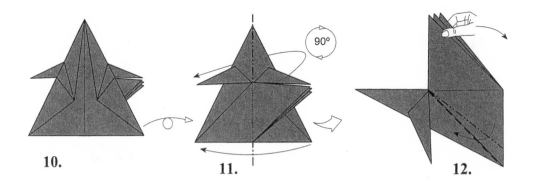

10.

11.

12.

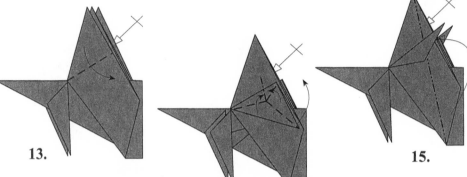

13.

14.

15.

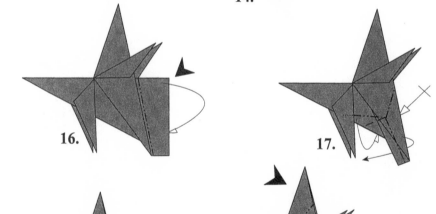

16.

17.

18.

19.

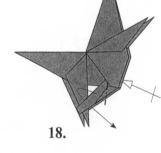

30

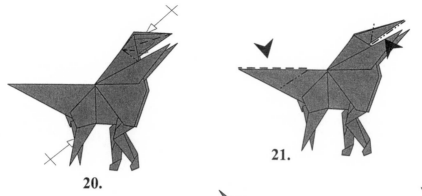

20.

21.

22.

23.

24.

25.

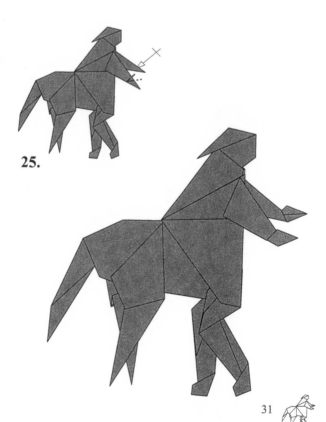

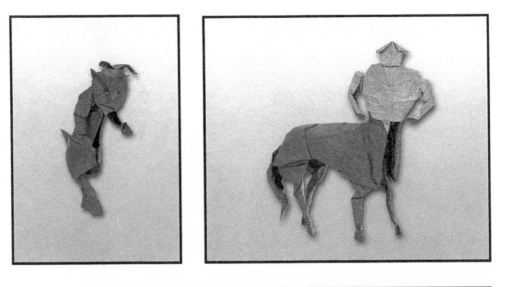

Part 2

Flying Serpent

After the fall and disappearance (extinction) of the "Draco Nobilis," this species was able to evolve and spread itself throughout the world.

Without being excessively dangerous, it could occasionally attack very aggressively.

Author: Mario Adrados Netto

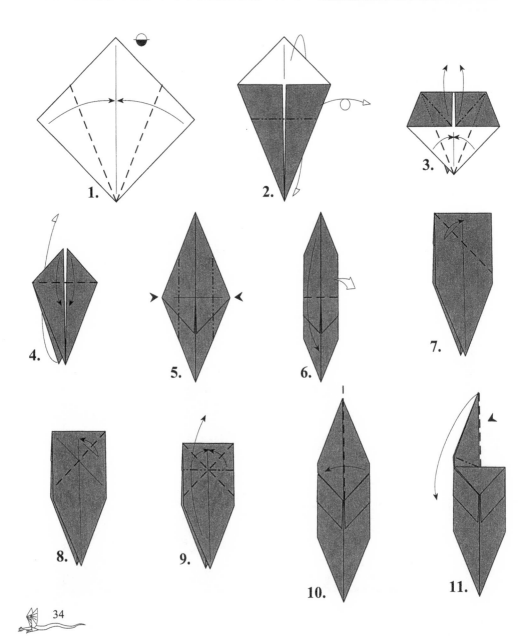

1.

2.

3.

4.

5.

6.

7.

8.

9.

10.

11.

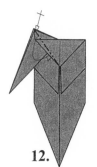

12.

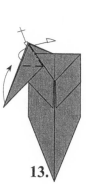

13.

14.

15.

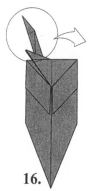

16.

17.

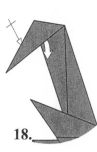

18.

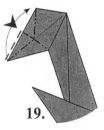

19.

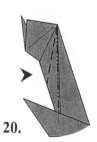

20.

21.

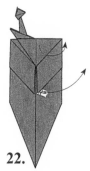

22.

23.

24.

25.

26.

22.25

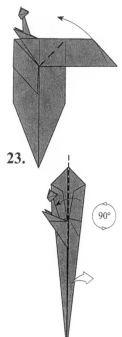

27.

90°

35

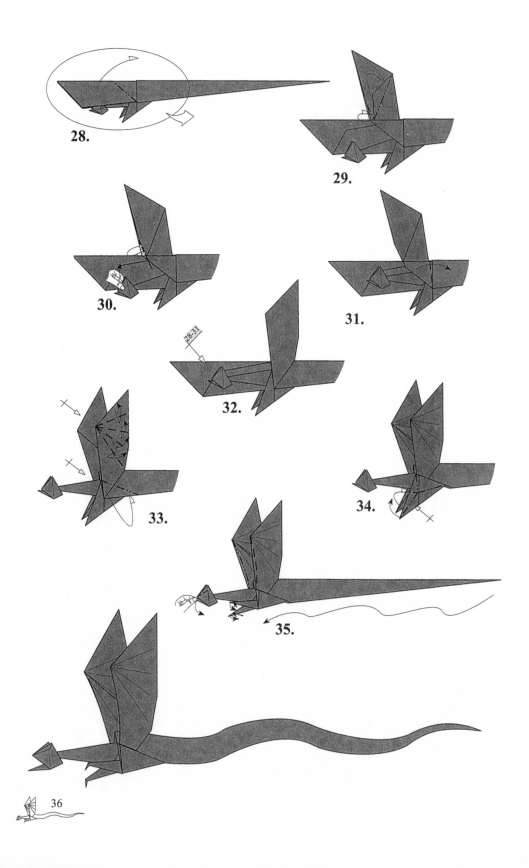

28.

29.

30.

31.

32.

33.

34.

35.

36

Demon

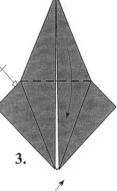

In the hierarchy of hell, the lowest rank is occupied by these demons. These are tortured souls who do the dirtiest work in exchange for a postponement of their punishment.

Authors: Mario Adrados - J. Aníbal Voyer

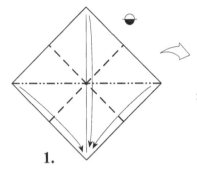

1.

2.

3.

4.

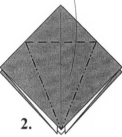

5.

6.

7.

8.

9. Repeat 6–8 on the three other points.

90°

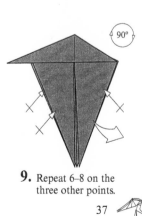

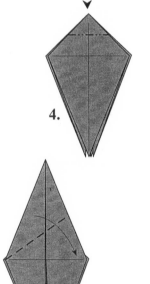
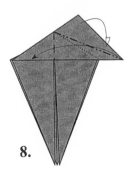

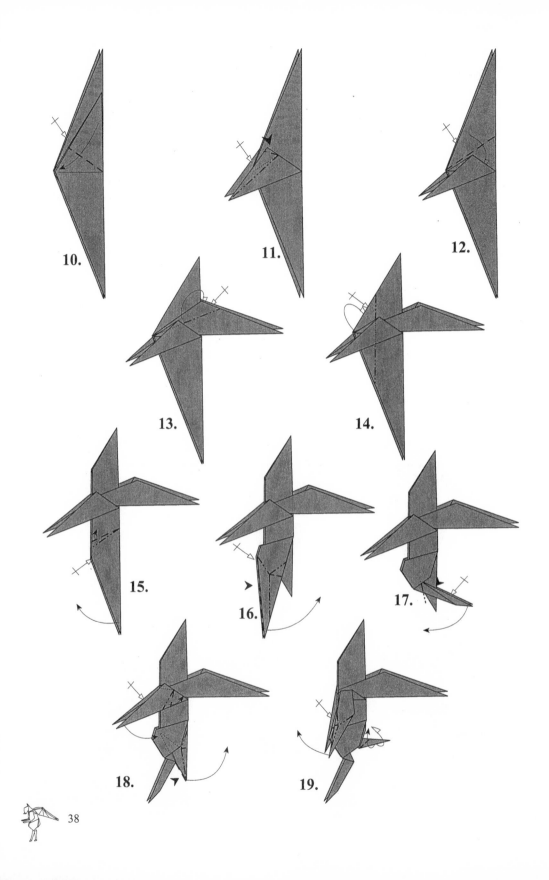

10.

11.

12.

13.

14.

15.

16.

17.

18.

19.

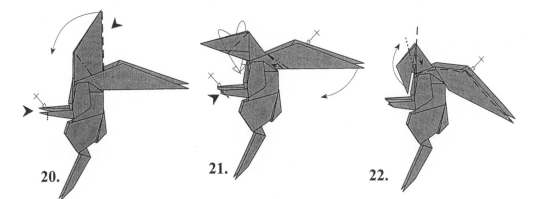

20.

21.

22.

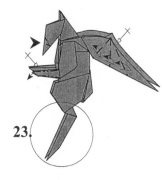

23.

24.

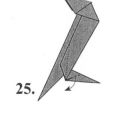

25.

26.

27.

28.

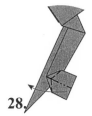

29.

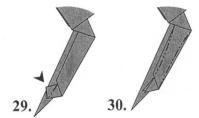

30.

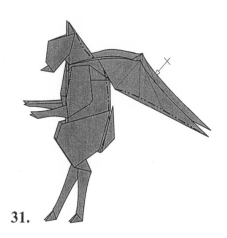

31.

Griffin

Half-lion, half-eagle, the Griffin was very superior in size to both of these two animals. It had the body and tail of a lion, but was eight times bigger. It possessed the head and wings of an eagle, but was a thousand times stronger. It was thought that this strange creature lived in the mountains, where it would swoop down over its prey. With its powerful talons, it was capable of carrying very large prey to its nest—even a horse, with its rider included.

Author: Mario Adrados Netto

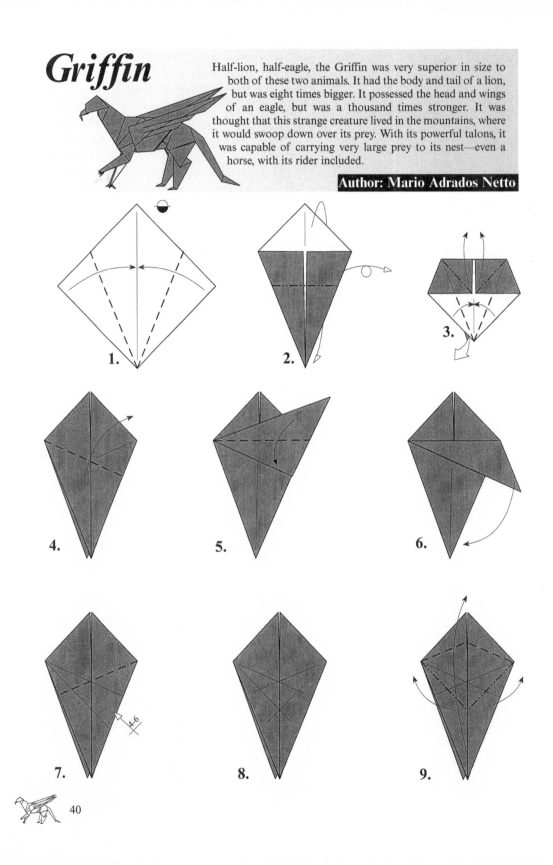

1.

2.

3.

4.

5.

6.

7.

8.

9.

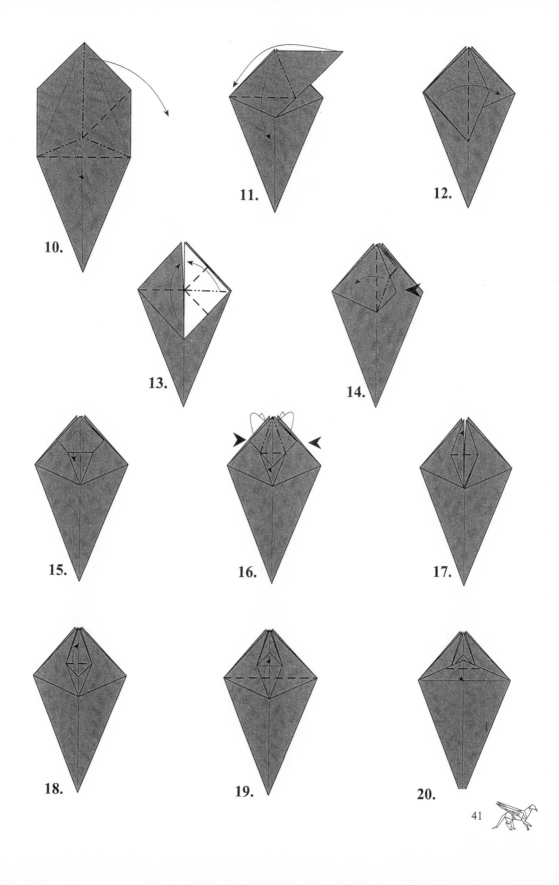

10.

11.

12.

13.

14.

15.

16.

17.

18.

19.

20.

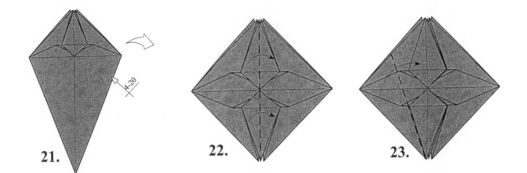

21.

22.

23.

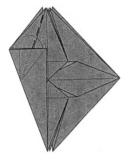

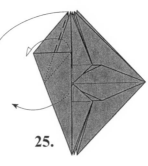

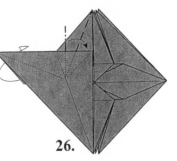

25.

26.

24. Fold one layer.

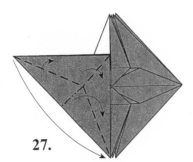

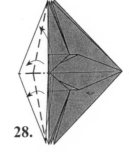

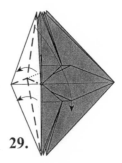

27.

28.

29.

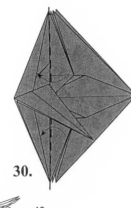

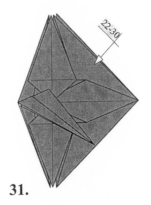

30.

31.

32.

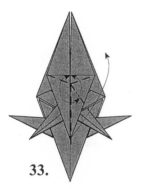

33.

34.

35.

36.

37.

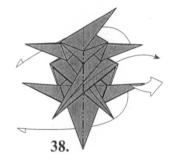

38.

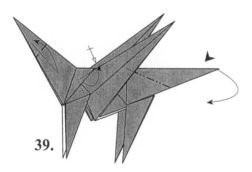

39.

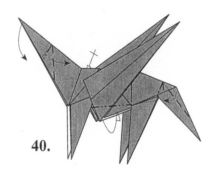

40.

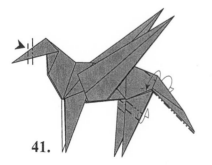

41.

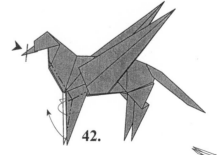

42.

43

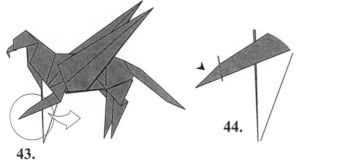

43.

44.

45.

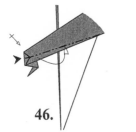

46.

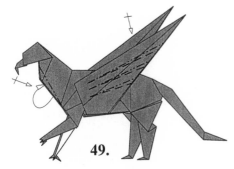

47.

48.
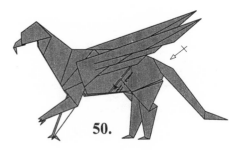

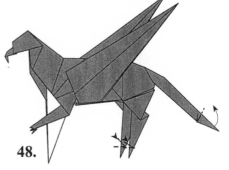

49.

50.

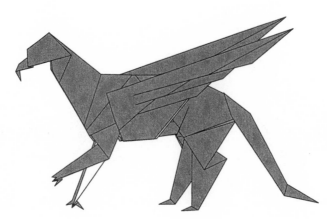

Cerberus

This mythological monster was the son of Typhon and Echinda. According to legend, Cerberus was a three-headed dog who guarded the doors to Hades, the subterranean region or hell of Greek mythology. This creature would not let any living being in or out.

Author: Mario Adrados Netto

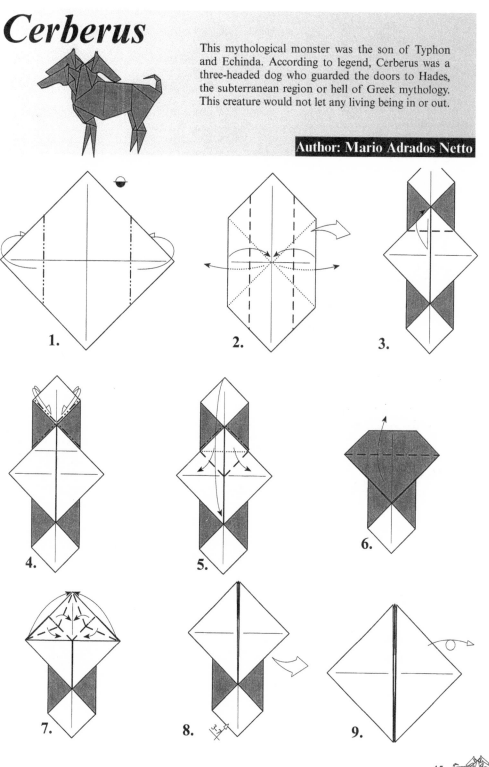

45

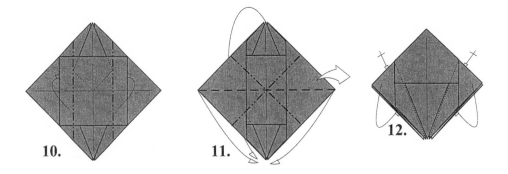

10.

11.

12.

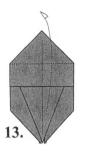

13.

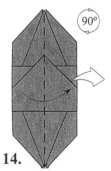

14.

90°

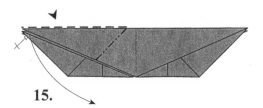

15.

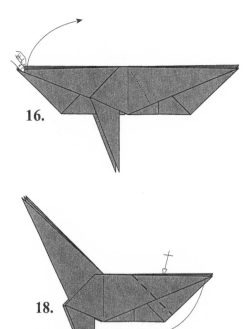

16.

18.

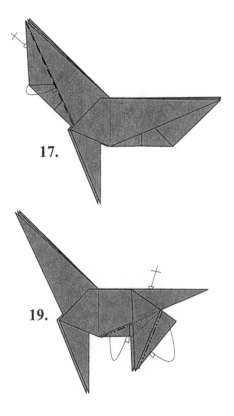

17.

19.

46

20.

21.

22.

19-20

23.

24.

25.

26.

27.

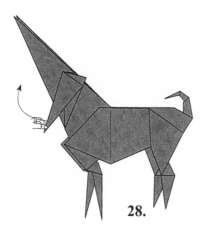

28.

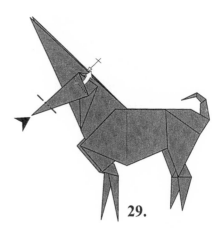

29.

30.

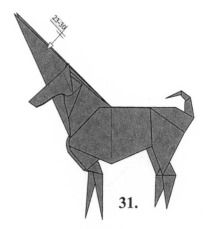

23.30

31.

Wizard

Wizards are more than humans, but less than gods. They are united with the forces of nature, air, water, earth, and fire. They claim to be spiritual guides to tribes and kingdoms, attracting or distancing them from the light, according to their inclinations.

Author: J. Aníbal Voyer Iniesta

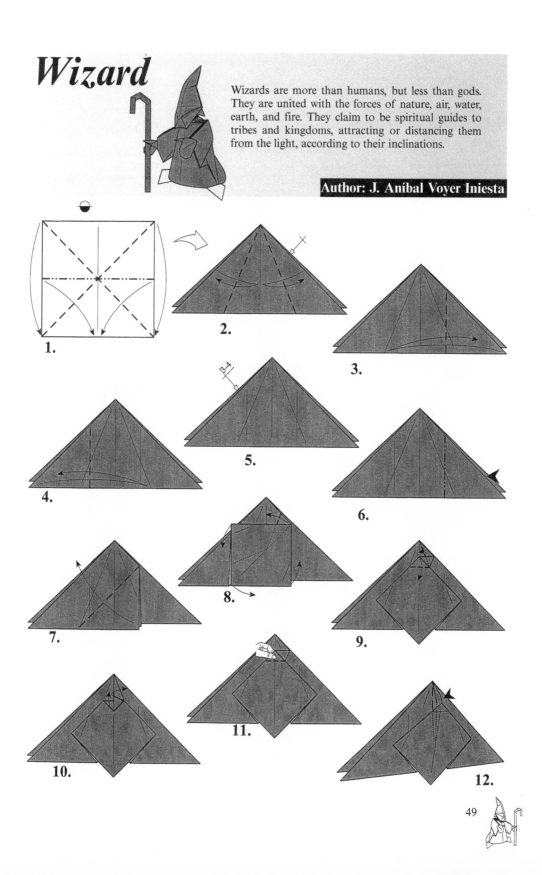

1.

2.

3.

4.

5.

6.

7.

8.

9.

10.

11.

12.

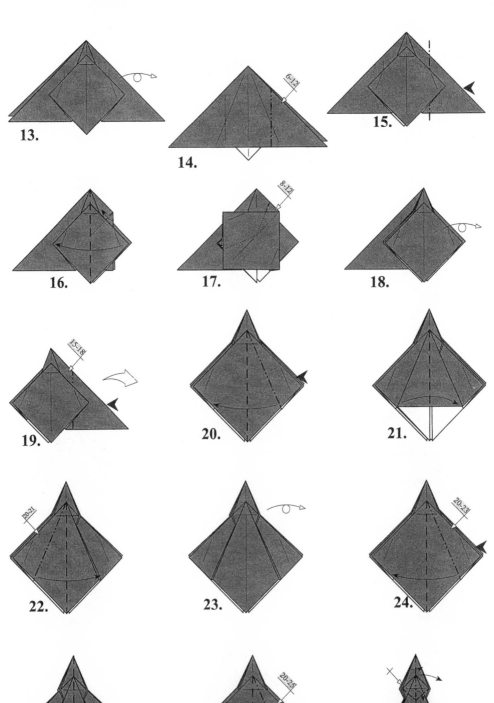

13.

14. 6-12

15.

16.

17. 8-12

18.

19. 15-18

20.

21.

22. 20-21

23.

24. 20-23

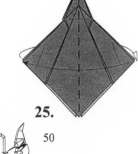

25.

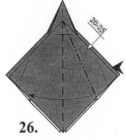

26. 20-25

27.

50

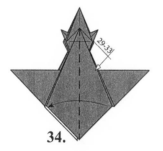

28.

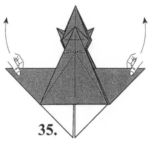

29.

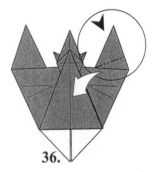

30.

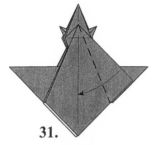

31.

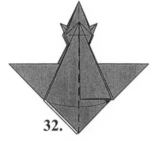

32.

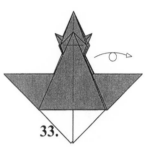

33.

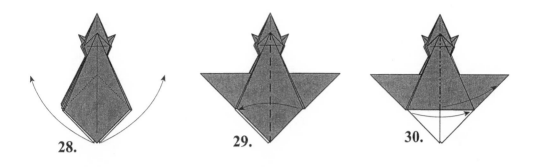

29-33

34.

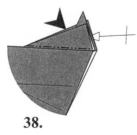

35.

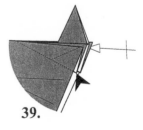

36.

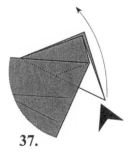

37.

38.

39.

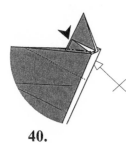

40.

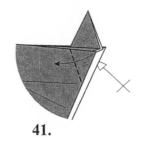

41.

42.

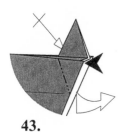

43.

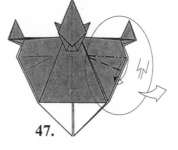

44.

45.

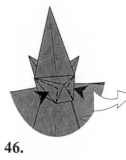

46.

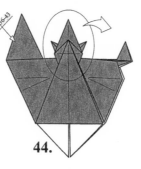

47.

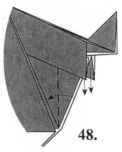

48.

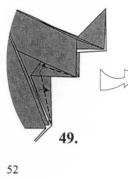

49.

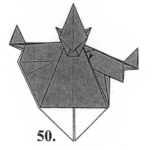

50.

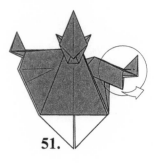

51.

52.

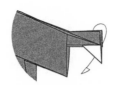

53.

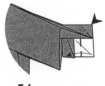

54.

55.

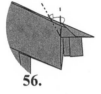

56.

57.

58.

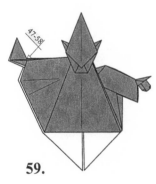

59.

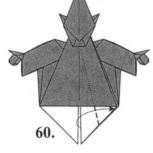

60.

61.

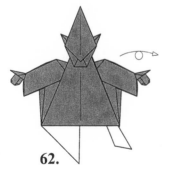

62.

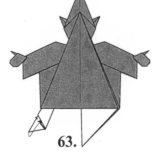

63.

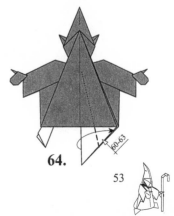

64.

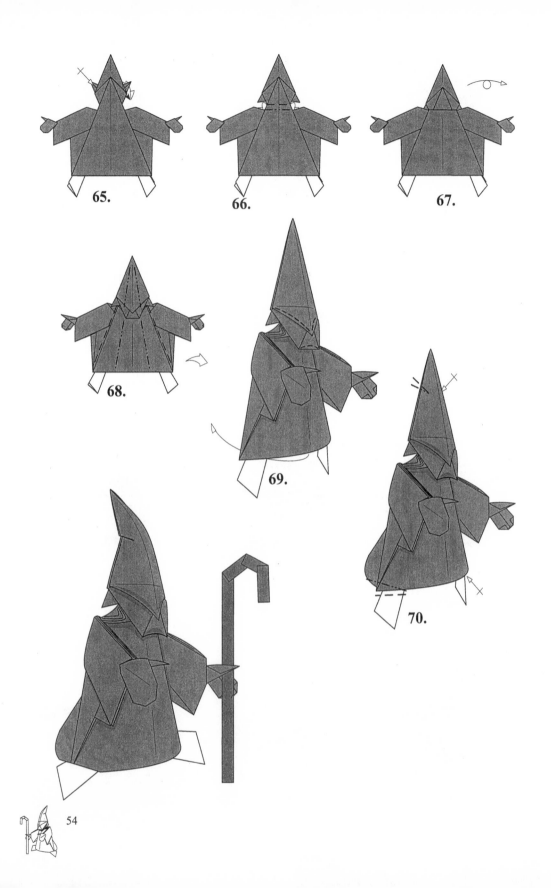

65.

66.

67.

68.

69.

70.

Satyr

These are mythological beings, half-man and half-goat, who represent the vital forces of nature in their plenitude. Peloponnesia and probably Arcadia, seem to have been their country of origin. The pastoral regions of Arcadia had once been centers of worship of the cult of Pan (the divine "goat foot") since antiquity.

Authors: Mario Adrados - J. Aníbal Voyer

1.

2.

3.

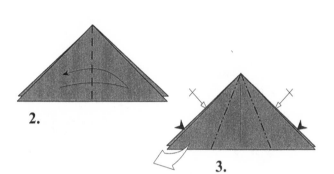

4.

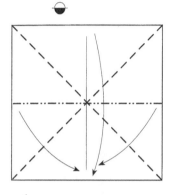

5.

6.

7.

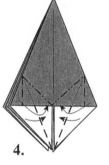

8.

9.

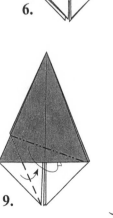

55

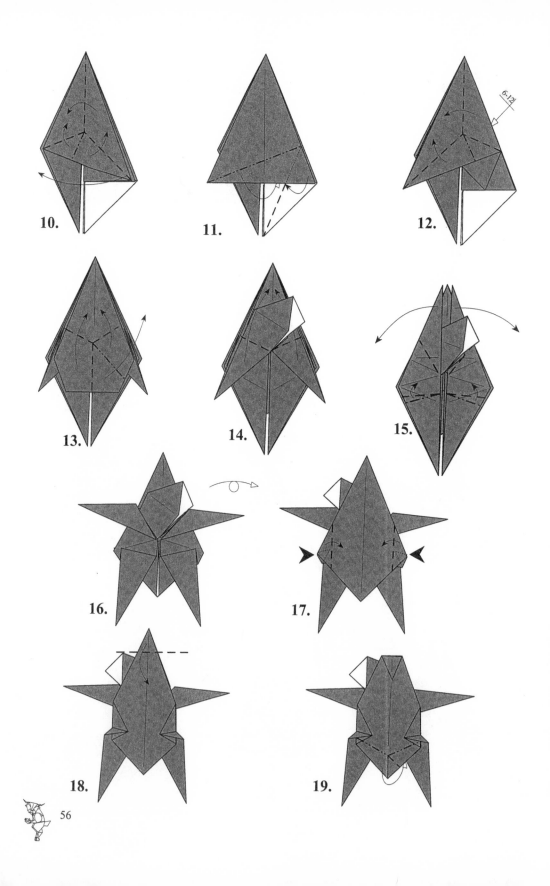

10.

11.

12.

13.

14.

15.

16.

17.

18.

19.

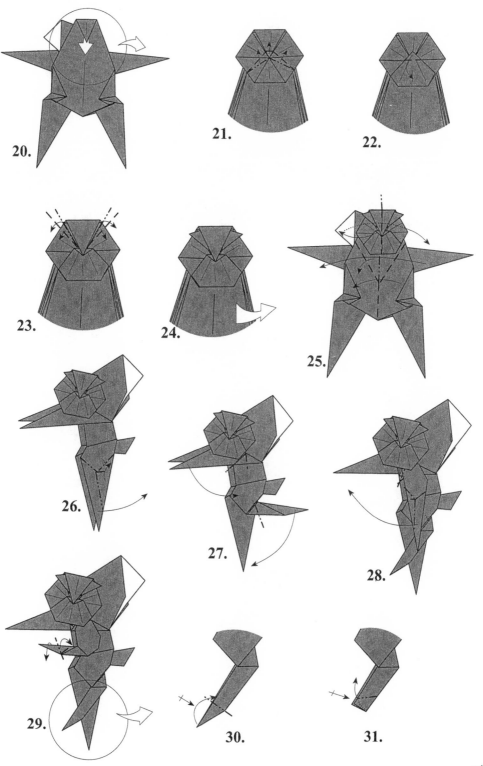

20.

21.

22.

23.

24.

25.

26.

27.

28.

29.

30.

31.

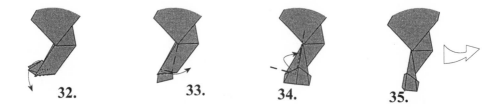

32. **33.** **34.** **35.**

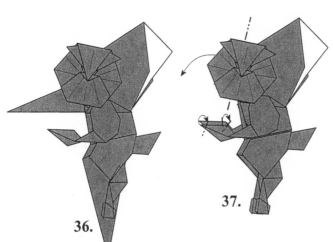

36.

37.

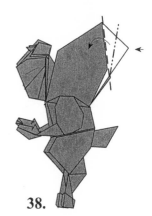

38.

39.

40. **41.**

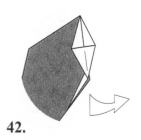

42.

43. **44.**

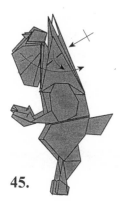

45.

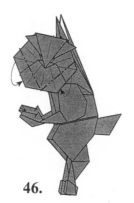

46.

47.

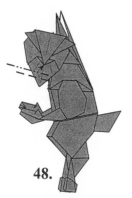

48.

49.

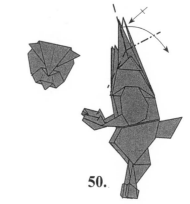

50.

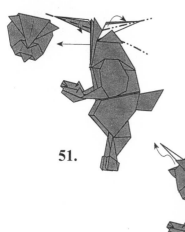

51.

52.

59

Unicorn

This animal of fable is a symbol of virginity and of religion. Greek and Roman authors cite the unicorn as originating in India. It had the form of a horse and a solitary horn, long and sharp on its forehead. The body was white, and it had a red head and blue eyes. It was noted for its strength, agility, and ferocity.

Author: Mario Adrados Netto

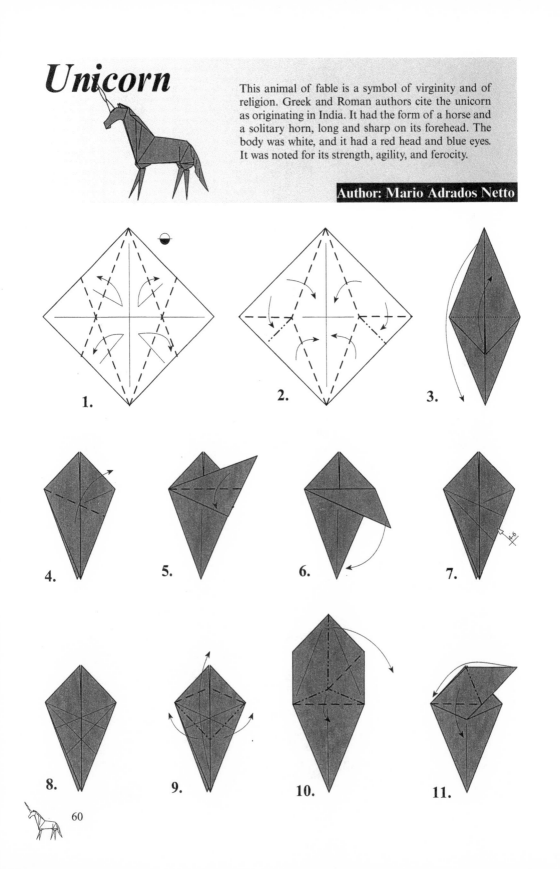

1.

2.

3.

4.

5.

6.

7.

8.

9.

10.

11.

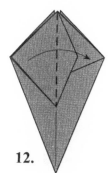

12.

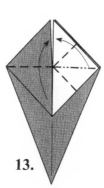

13.

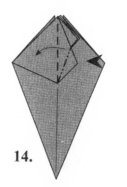

14.

15.

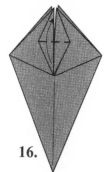

16.

17.

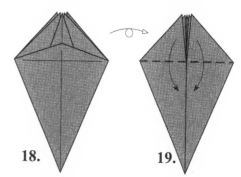

18.

19.

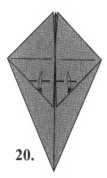

20.

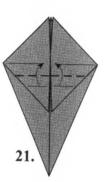

21.

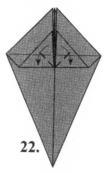

22.

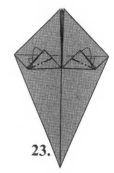

23.

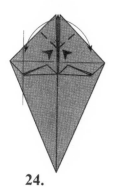

24.

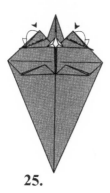

25.

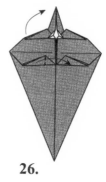

26.

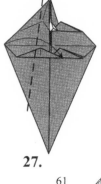

27.

61

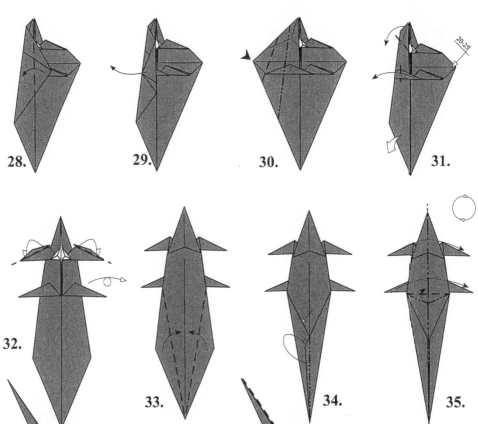

28.

29.

30.

31.

32.

33.

34.

35.

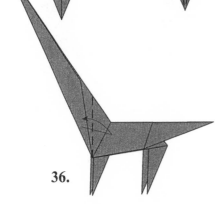

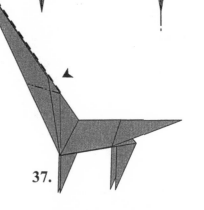

36.

37.

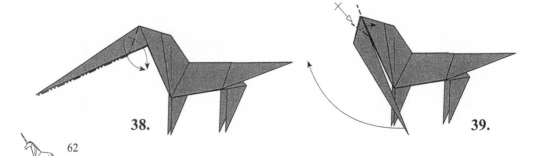

38.

39.

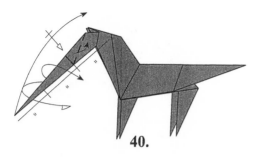

40.

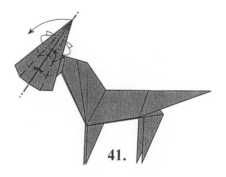

41.

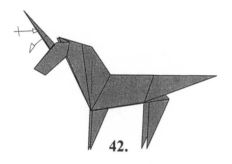

42.

43.

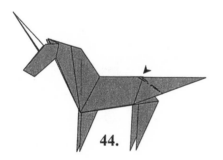

44.

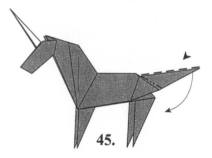

45.

46.

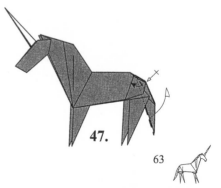

47.

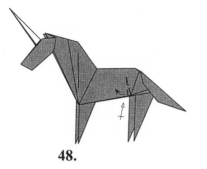

48.

49.

50.

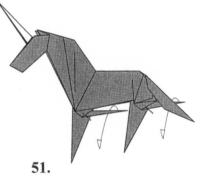

51.

52. Repeat on the two other legs.

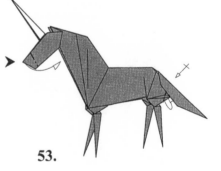

53.

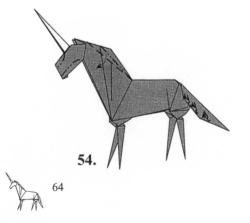

54.

55.

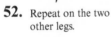

56.

57.

58.

59.

60.

61.

62.

63.

64.

65.

66.

67.

Sphinx

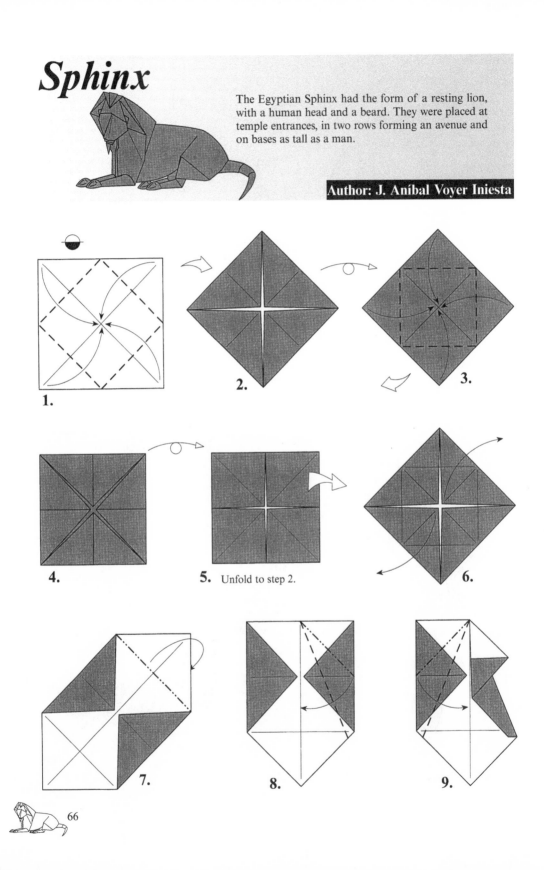

The Egyptian Sphinx had the form of a resting lion, with a human head and a beard. They were placed at temple entrances, in two rows forming an avenue and on bases as tall as a man.

Author: J. Aníbal Voyer Iniesta

1.

2.

3.

4.

5. Unfold to step 2.

6.

7.

8.

9.

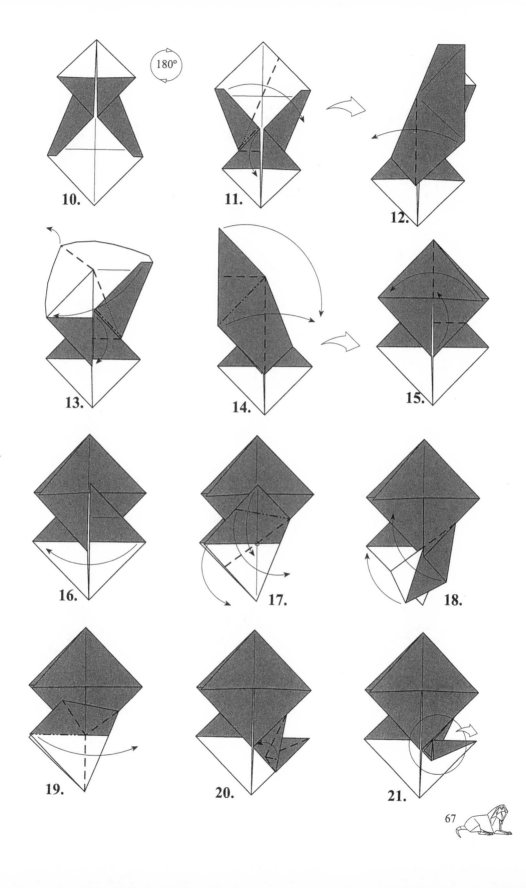

10.

180°

11.

12.

13.

14.

15.

16.

17.

18.

19.

20.

21.

67

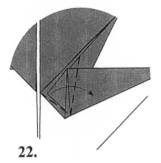

22.

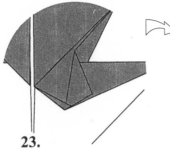

23.

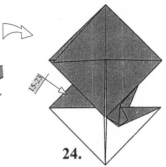

15-23

24.

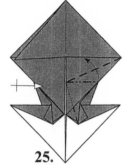

25.

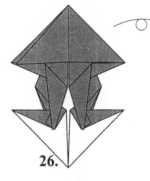

26.

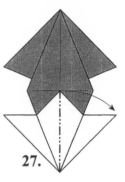

27.

28.

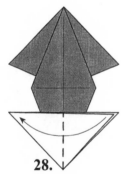

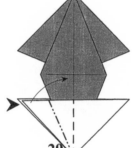

29.

30.

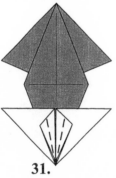

31.

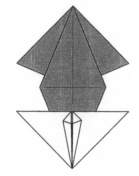

32. Unfold to step 29.

33.

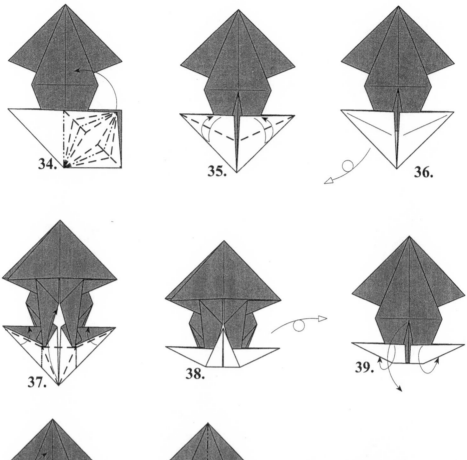

34.

35.

36.

37.

38.

39.

40.

41.

42.

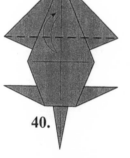

43.

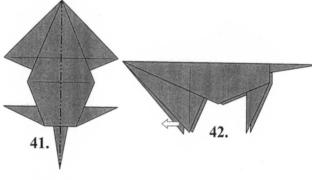

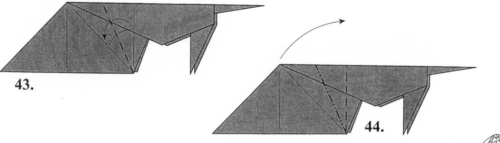

44.

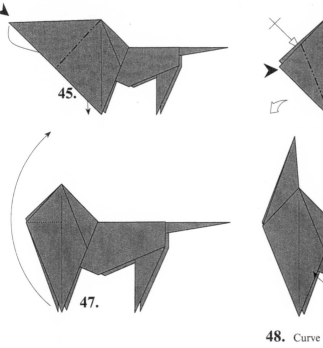

45.

46.

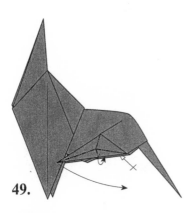

47.

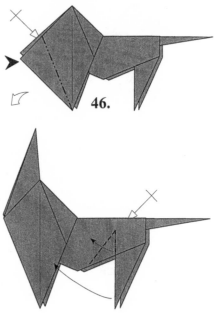

48. Curve the figure as you fold it.

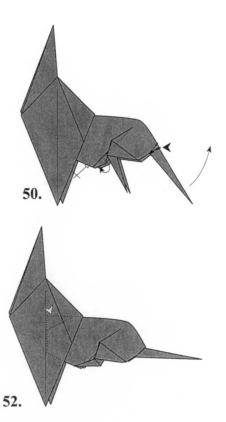

49.

50.

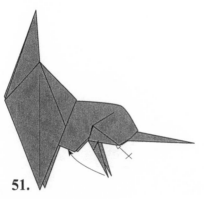

51.

52.

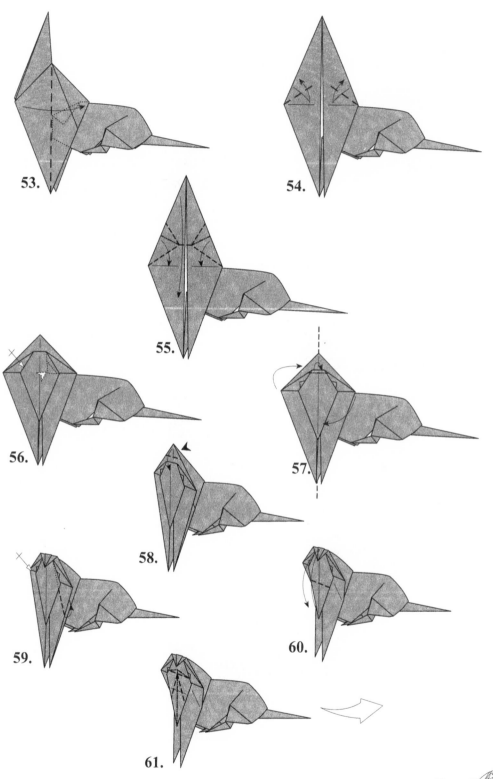

53.

54.

55.

56.

57.

58.

59.

60.

61.

71

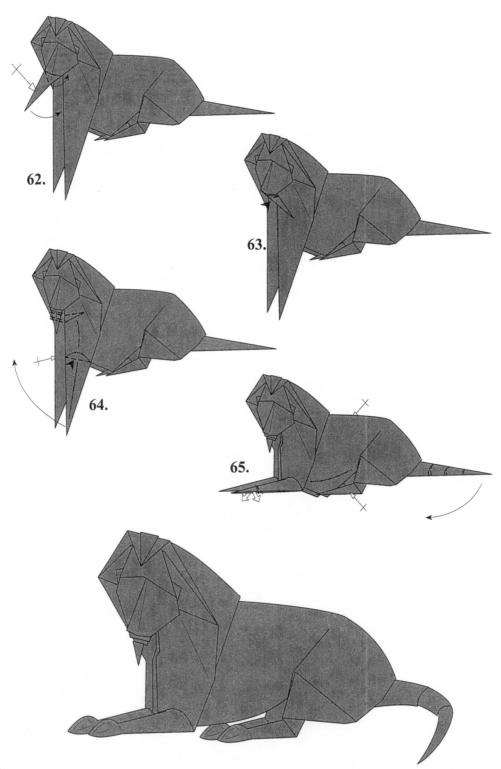

62.

63.

64.

65.

Centaur

According to more extended traditions in Greece, centaurs are considered to be the sons of Nephele (cloud goddess) and Ixion. Ixion, who was accused of the death of his father-in-law, was absolved by Zeus and seated at his celestial table. Responding to this hospitality, he declared his love for Hera. Zeus became irritated and sent a cloud in the form of Hera to Ixion, fooling him, and from that union was born the Centaur.

Author: Mario Adrados Netto

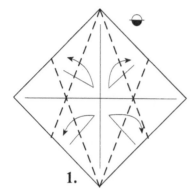

1.

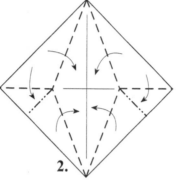

2.

3.

4.

5.

6.

7.

8.

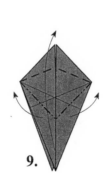

9.

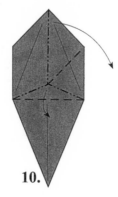

10.

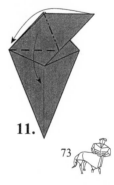

11.

73

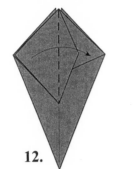

12.

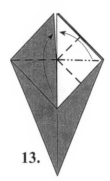

13.

14.

15.

16.

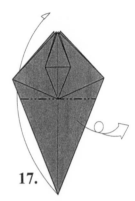

17.

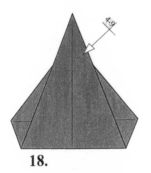

18.

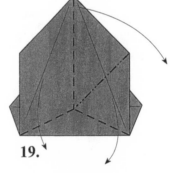

19.

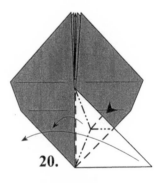

20.

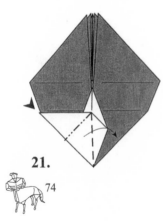

21.

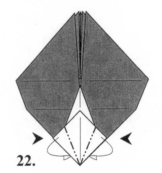

22.

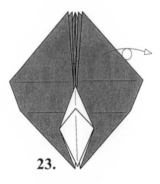

23.

74

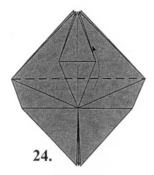

24.

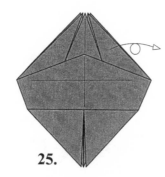

25.

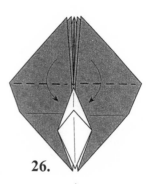

26.

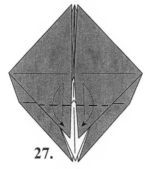

27.

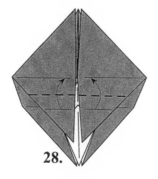

28.

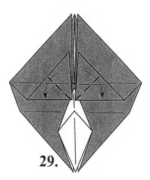

29.

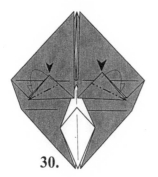

30.

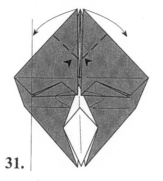

31.

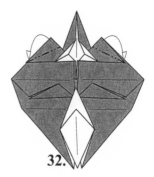

32.

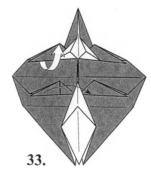

33.

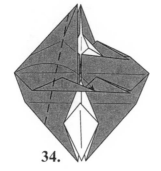

34.

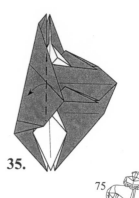

35.

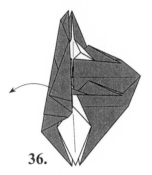

36.

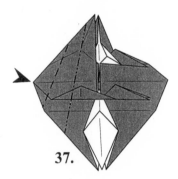

37.

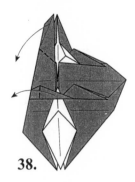

38.

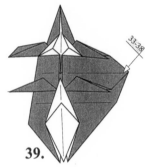

39.

33-38

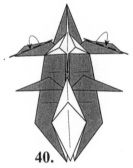

40.

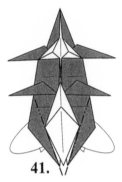

41.

180°

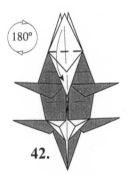

42.

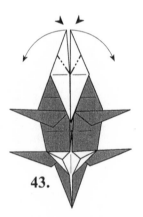

43.

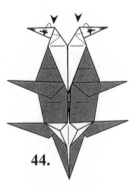

44.

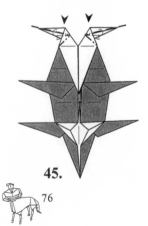

45.

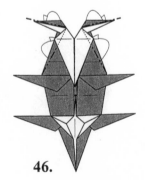

46.

47.

76

48.

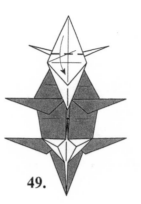

49.

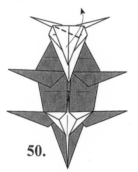

50.

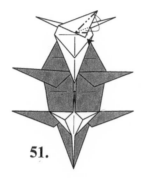

51.

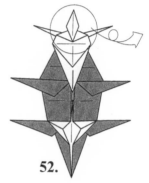

52.

53.

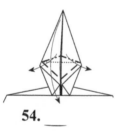

54.

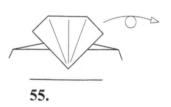

55.

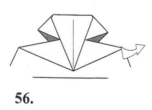

56.

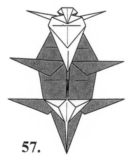

57.

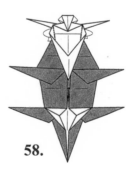

58.

77

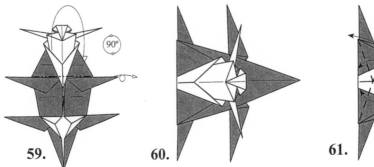

59. 90°

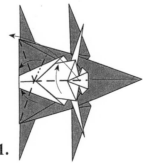

60.

61.

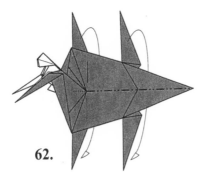

62.

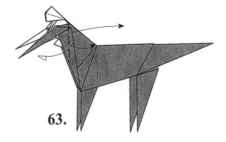

63.

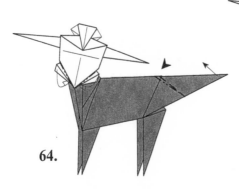

64.

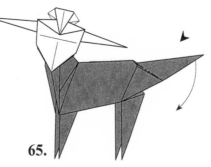

65.

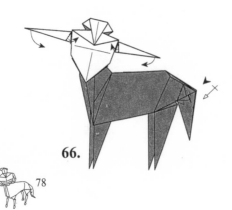

66.

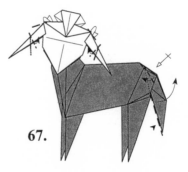

67.

68. Make the body three-dimensional.

69. Stretch the front legs out a little.

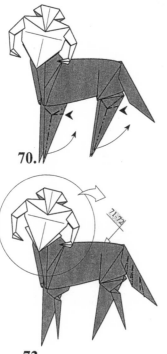

70.

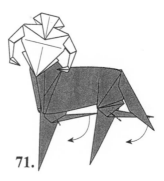

71.

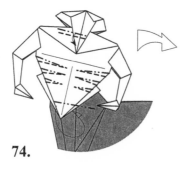

72.

73. Make the head three-dimensional.

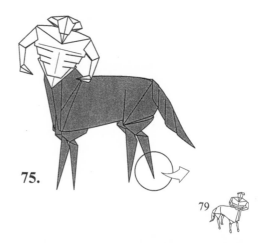

74.

75.

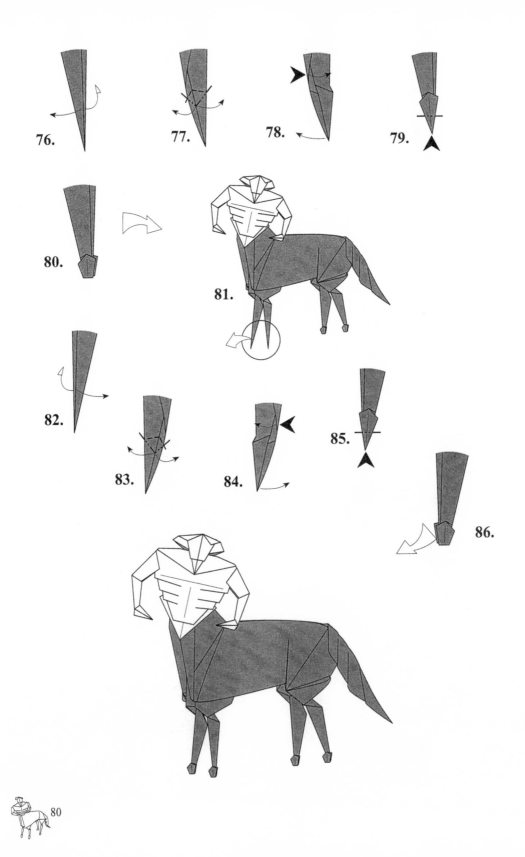

76.

77.

78.

79.

80.

81.

82.

83.

84.

85.

86.

Recommendations:

1. It is very important to use fine paper, preferably metallic, so that it will maintain the shape better.
2. The smallest size paper should be more than 25 cm.
3. The best results are obtained using compound papers. These can be made by glueing colorful tissue wrapping paper and aluminum foil. The tissue paper represents the side shown for the finished model.

Part 3

Lady

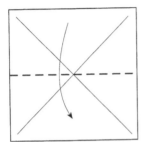

Lorelei the Beautiful was disfigured during the assault on Grand Castle and she swore she would do anything to recover her beauty. Mephistopheles heard her and offered her a bargain. He would return her beauty in exchange for her companionship...*Forever!*

Author: Mario Adrados Netto

1. Divide into 32.

2.

3. Take out a bit.

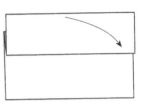

4.

5.

6.

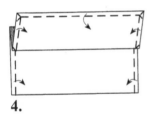

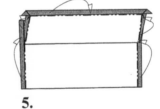

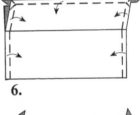

7.

8.

9.

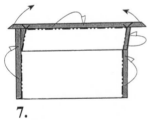

10.

11.

12.

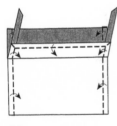

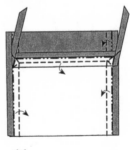

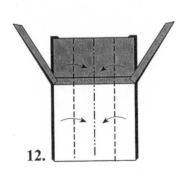

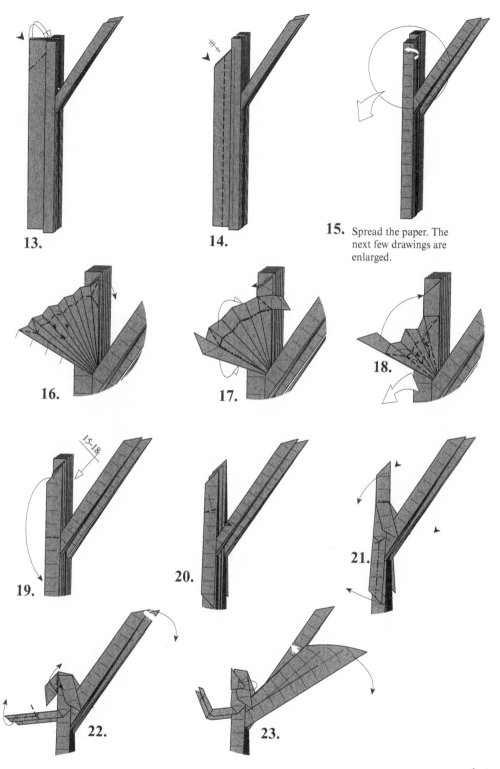

13.

14.

15. Spread the paper. The next few drawings are enlarged.

16.

17.

18.

19. 15-18

20.

21.

22.

23.

83

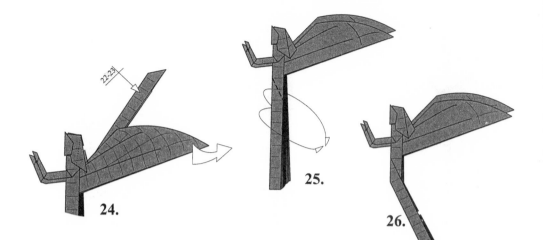

24.

25.

26.

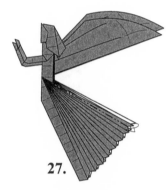

27.

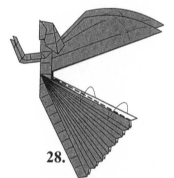

28.

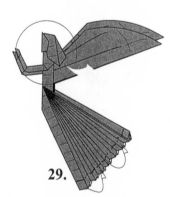

29.

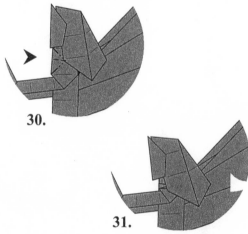

30.

31.

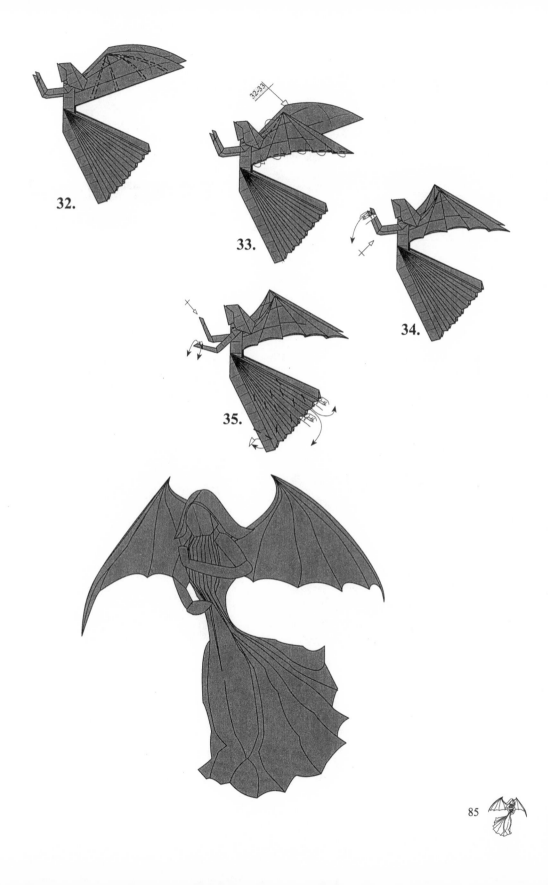

32.

33.

34.

35.

32-33!

Medusa

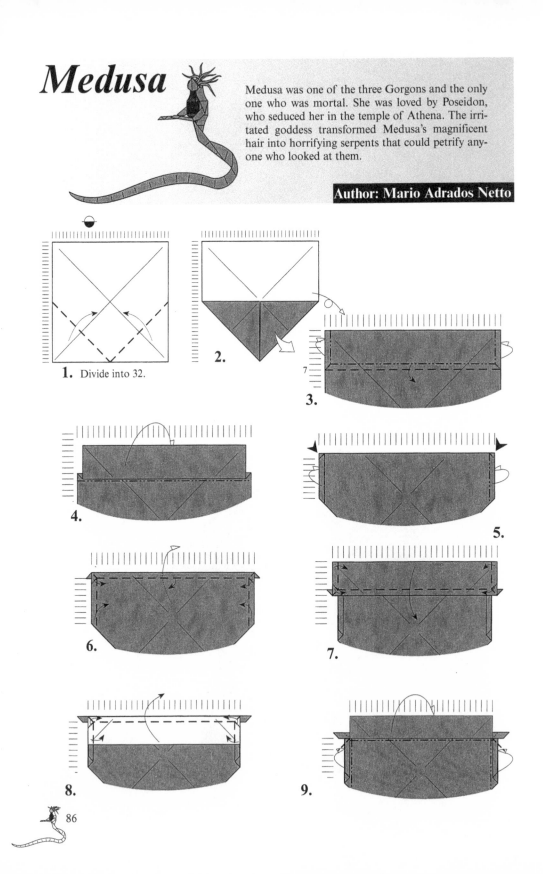

Medusa was one of the three Gorgons and the only one who was mortal. She was loved by Poseidon, who seduced her in the temple of Athena. The irritated goddess transformed Medusa's magnificent hair into horrifying serpents that could petrify anyone who looked at them.

Author: Mario Adrados Netto

1. Divide into 32.

2.

3.

4.

5.

6.

7.

8.

9.

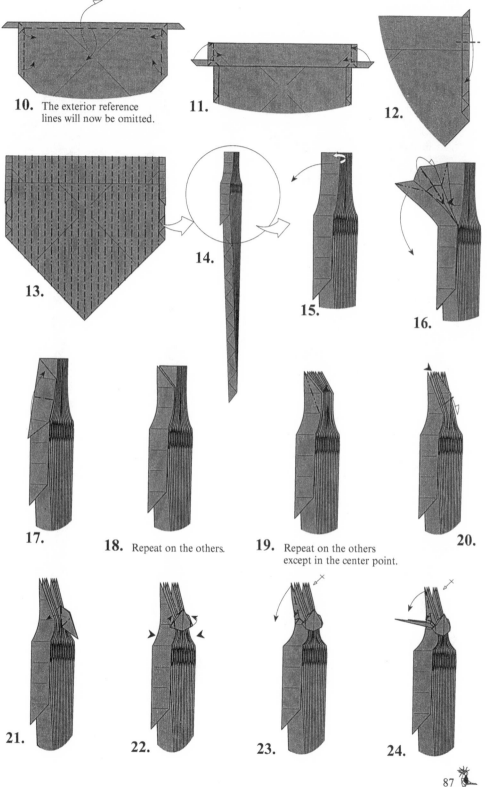

10. The exterior reference lines will now be omitted.

11.

12.

13.

14.

15.

16.

17.

18. Repeat on the others.

19. Repeat on the others except in the center point.

20.

21.

22.

23.

24.

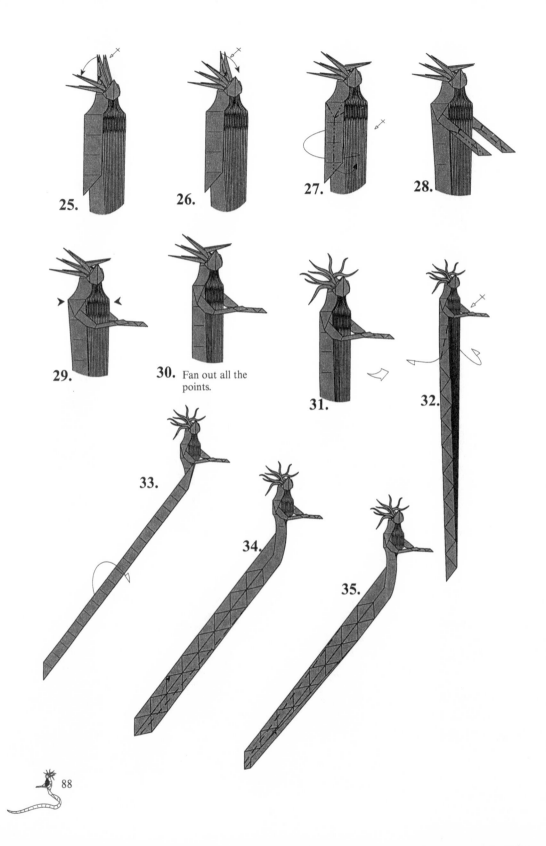

25.

26.

27.

28.

29.

30. Fan out all the
points.

31.

32.

33.

34.

35.

88

36.

37.

38.

Mephistopheles

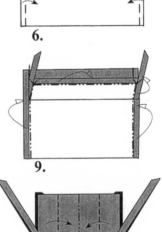

In the ancient Germanic legends, this infernal character appears as a companion of Dr. Faust with the name Mephistopheles. This current form has been generalized due to the influence of the work by Goethe. His etymology more likely extends from the origin of Megistophiel, Ophiel (from the Greek Ophis, meaning serpent), which was another name for Hermes Trismegistus, who in antiquity was the patron of wizards.

Author: Mario Adrados Netto

1. Divide into 32.

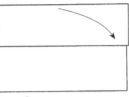

2.

3. Pull out a little.

4.

5.

6.

7.

8.

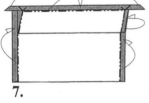

9.

10.

11.

12.

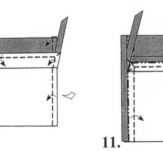

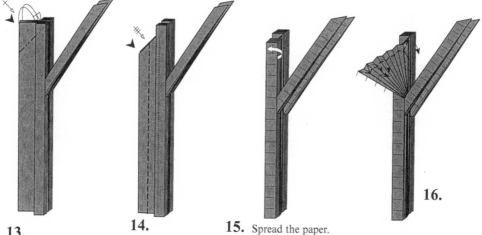

13.

14.

15. Spread the paper.

16.

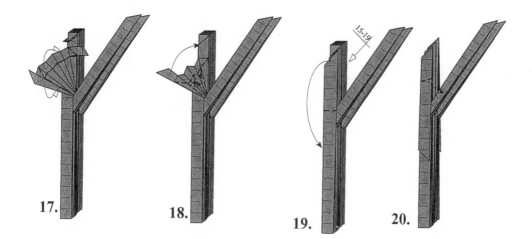

17.

18.

19.

20.

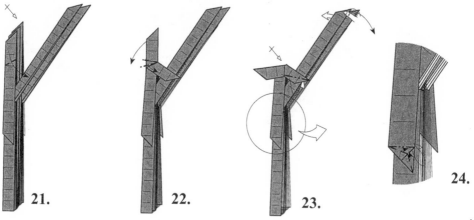

21.

22.

23.

24.

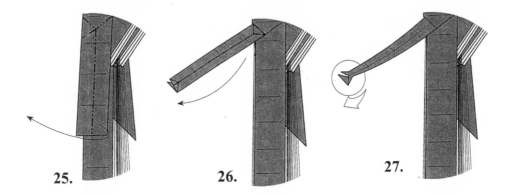

25. **26.** **27.**

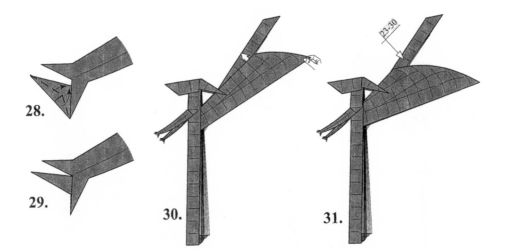

28.

29.

30. **31.**

23-30

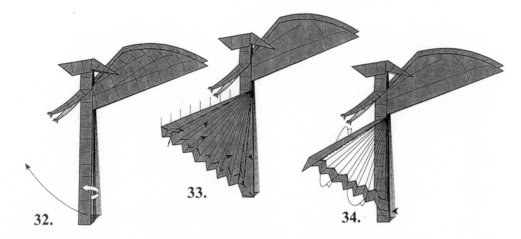

32. **33.** **34.**

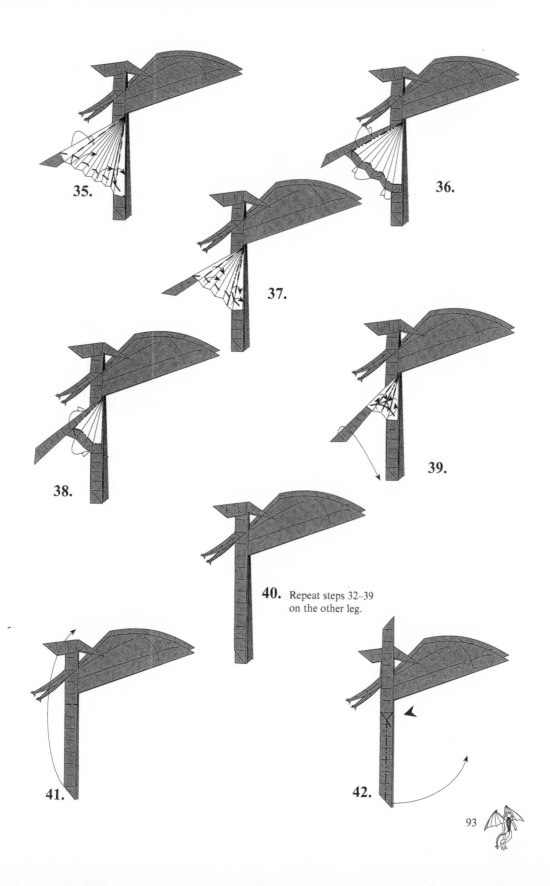

35.

36.

37.

38.

39.

40. Repeat steps 32–39 on the other leg.

41.

42.

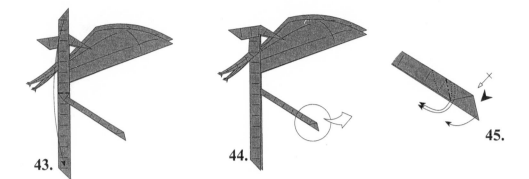

43.

44.

45.

46.

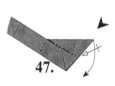

47.

48.

49.

50.

51.

52.

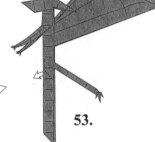

53.

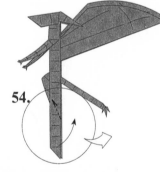

54.

55.

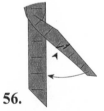

56.

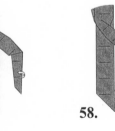

57.

58.

59.

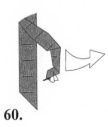

60.

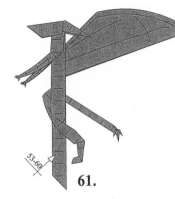

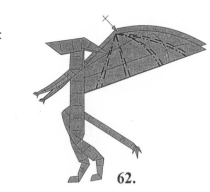

61.

62.

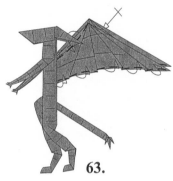

63.

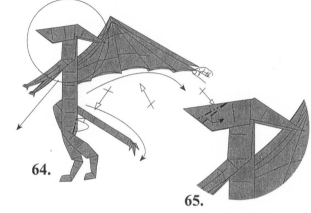

64.

65.

66.

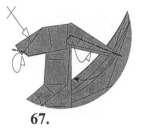

67.

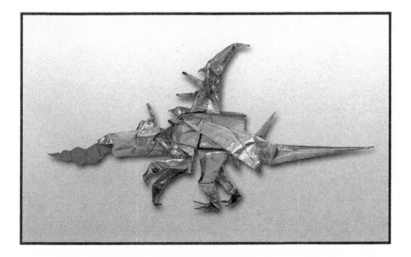

Part 4

Pegasus

This is the winged horse who was born of the blood of Medusa after having her head cut off by Perseus. The myth of Pegasus is closely related to that of Bellerophon, who, with the aid of the prodigious horse, conquered the Chimeara. But while intending to fly to the sky on his winged horse, he fell to earth, fracturing his leg. Pegasus, however, continued his flight, arriving at the sky, where he stayed among the stars.

Author: J. Aníbal Voyer Iniesta

1.

2.

3.

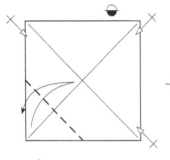

4.

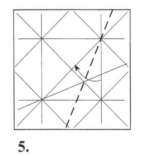

5.

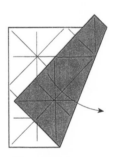

6.

7.

8.

9.

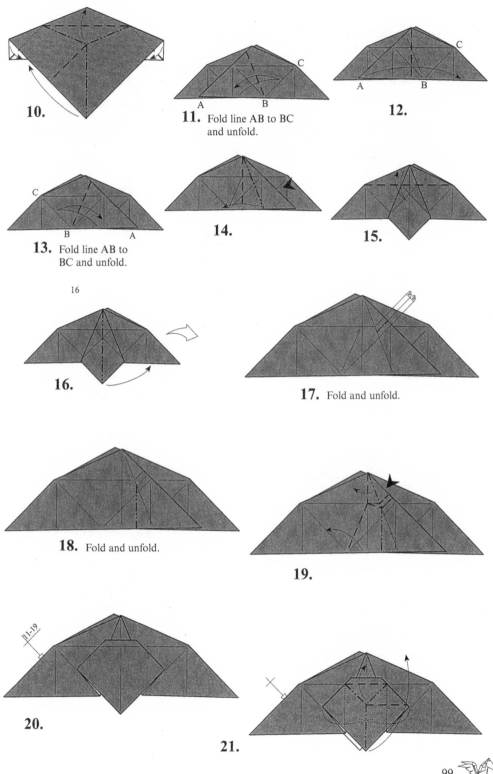

10.

11. Fold line AB to BC and unfold.

12.

13. Fold line AB to BC and unfold.

14.

15.

16

16.

17. Fold and unfold.

18. Fold and unfold.

19.

11-19

20.

21.

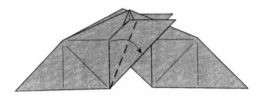

22.

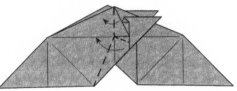

23.

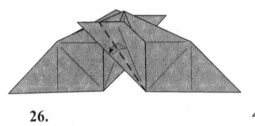

24.

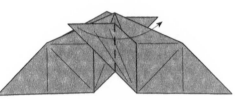

25.

26.

27.

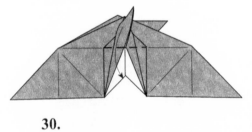

28.

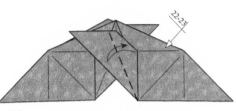

29. In this step the model cannot be left flat.

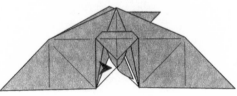

30.

31. Flatten the corner.

100

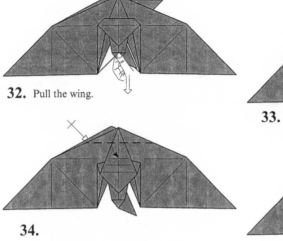

32. Pull the wing.

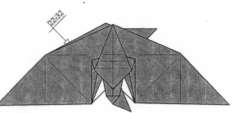

33.

34.

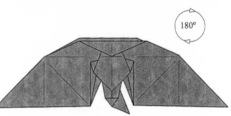

180°

35.

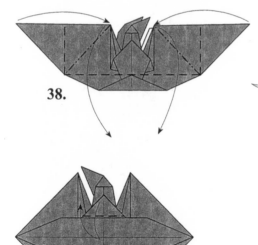

36.

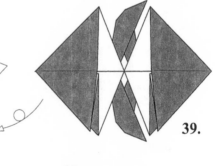

37.

38.

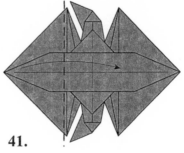

39.

40.

41.

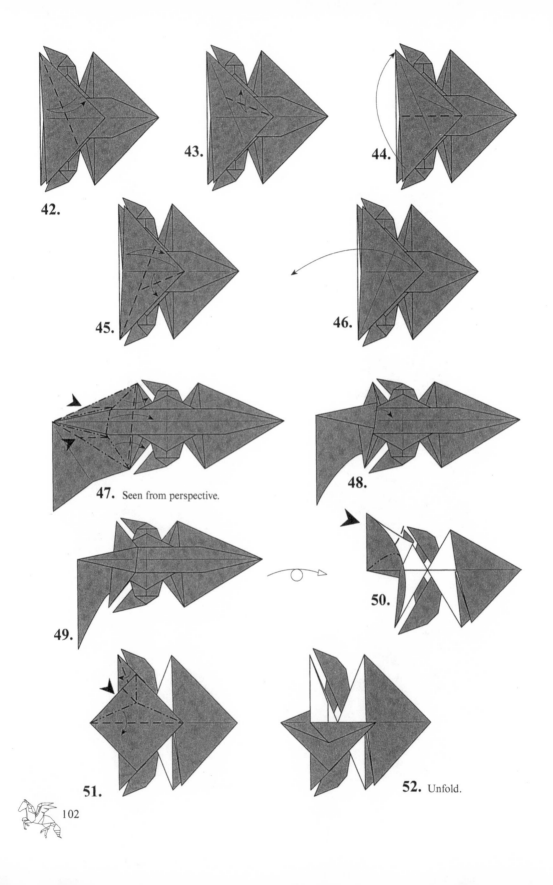

42.

43.

44.

45.

46.

47. Seen from perspective.

48.

49.

50.

51.

52. Unfold.

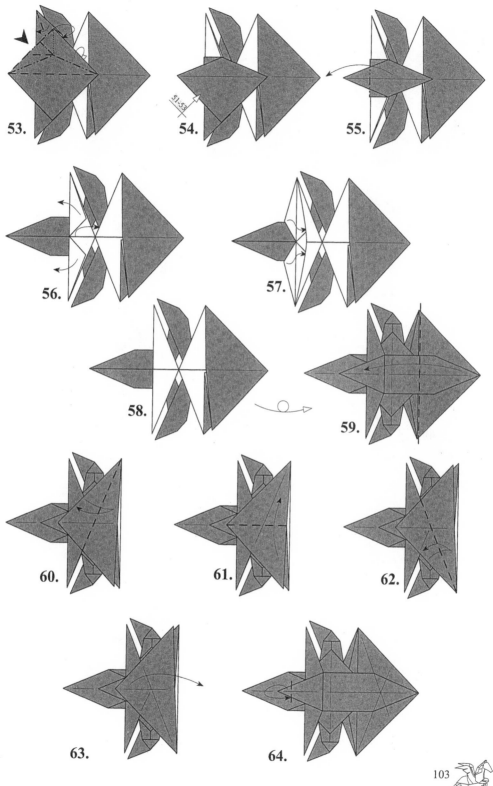

53.

54.

55.

56.

57.

58.

59.

60.

61.

62.

63.

64.

103

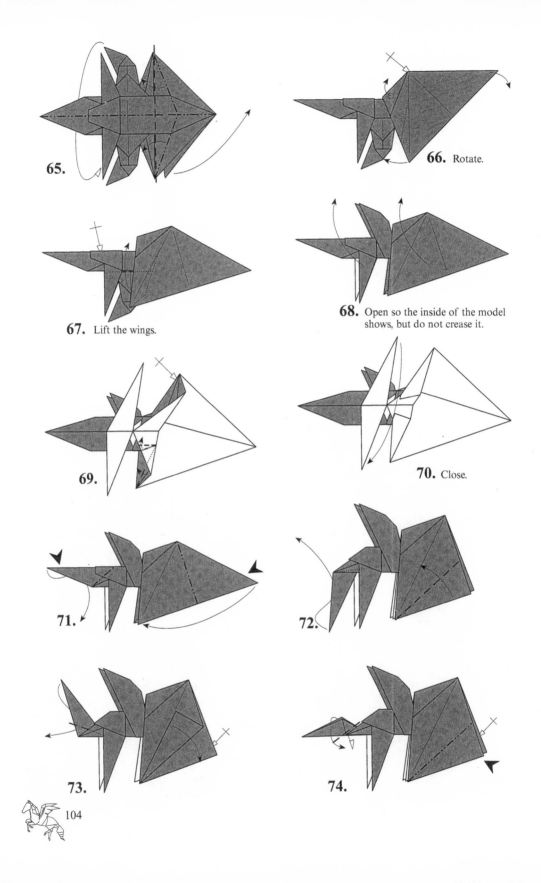

65.

66. Rotate.

67. Lift the wings.

68. Open so the inside of the model shows, but do not crease it.

69.

70. Close.

71.

72.

73.

74.

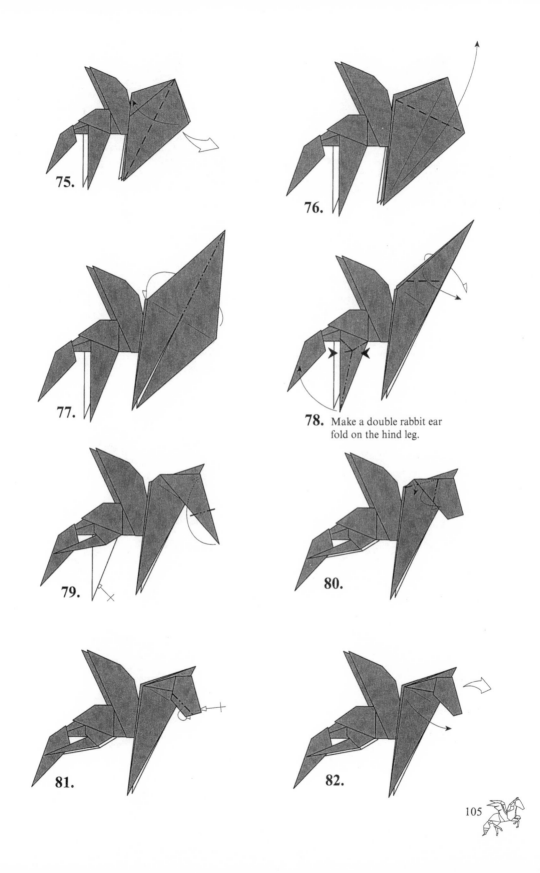

75.

76.

77.

78. Make a double rabbit ear fold on the hind leg.

79.

80.

81.

82.

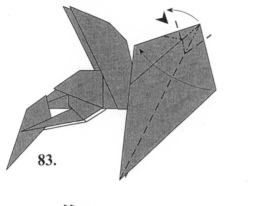

83.

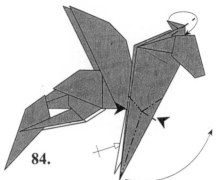

84.

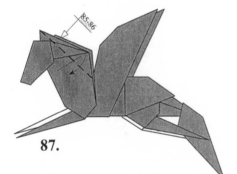

85.

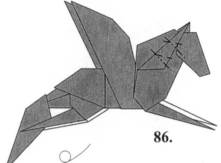

86.

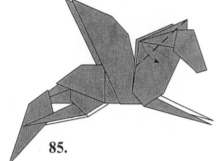

87.

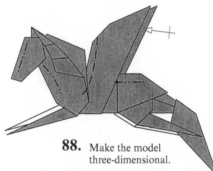

88. Make the model three-dimensional.

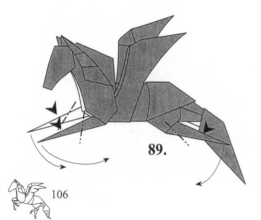

89.

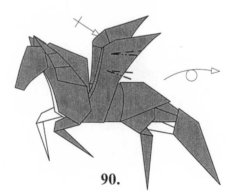

90.

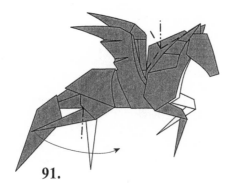

91.

92.

93.

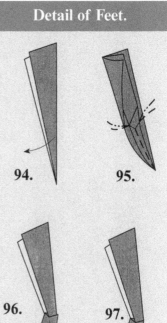

Detail of Feet.

94.

95.

96.

97.

Oriental Dragon

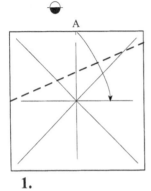

These dragons have the body of a serpent, short legs and no wings, yet they are still able to fly. In Chinese mythology, they are considered benefactors and extraordinarily long-lived and even immortal.

Author: J. Aníbal Voyer Iniesta

1.

2.

3.

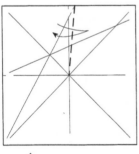

4.

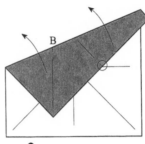

5.

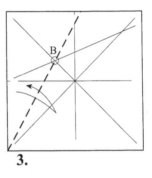

6.

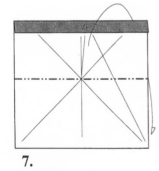

7.

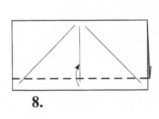

8.

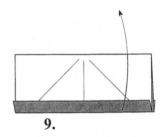

9.

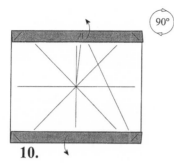

10.

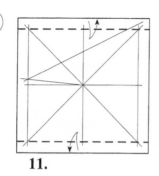

11.

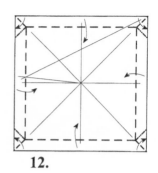

12.

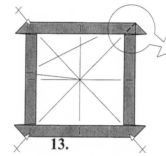

13.

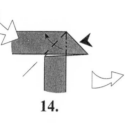

14.

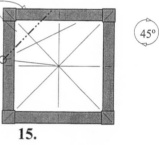

15.

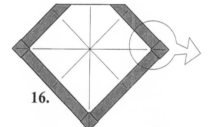

16.

17.

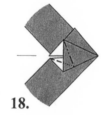

18.

19.

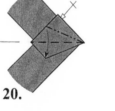

20.

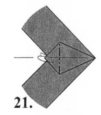

21.

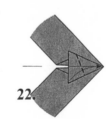

22.

23.

24.

25.

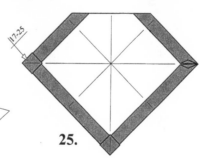

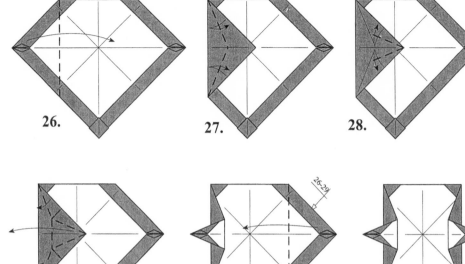

26.

27.

28.

29.

30. 26-29

31.

32.

33.

34.

35.

34-36

36.

37.

38.

39.

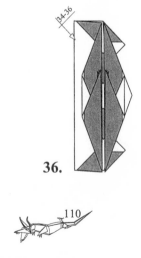110

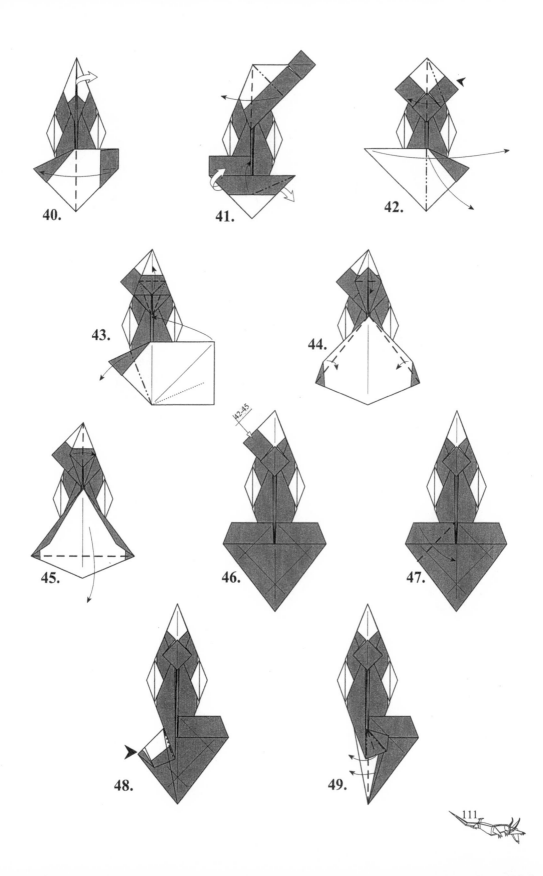

40.

41.

42.

43.

44.

45.

46.

47.

48.

49.

42-45

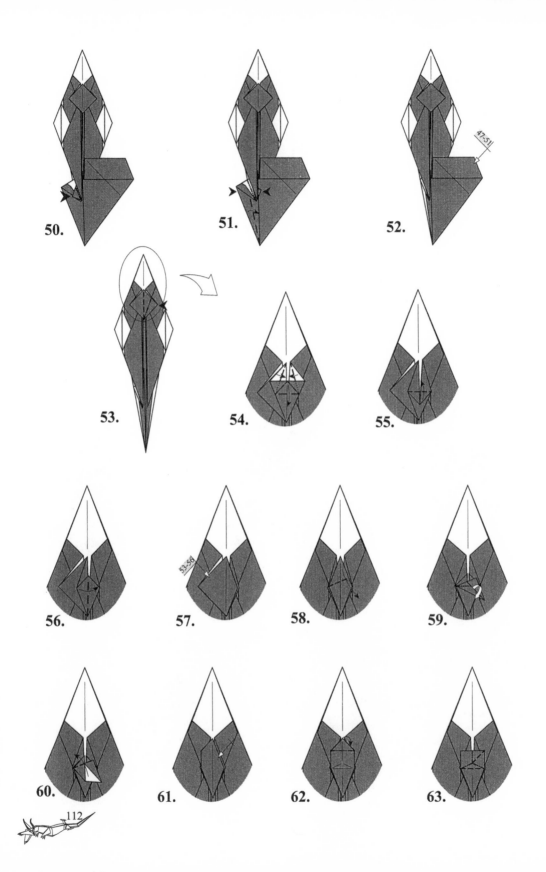

50.

51.

52. 47-51

53.

54.

55.

56.

57. 53-56

58.

59.

60.

112

61.

62.

63.

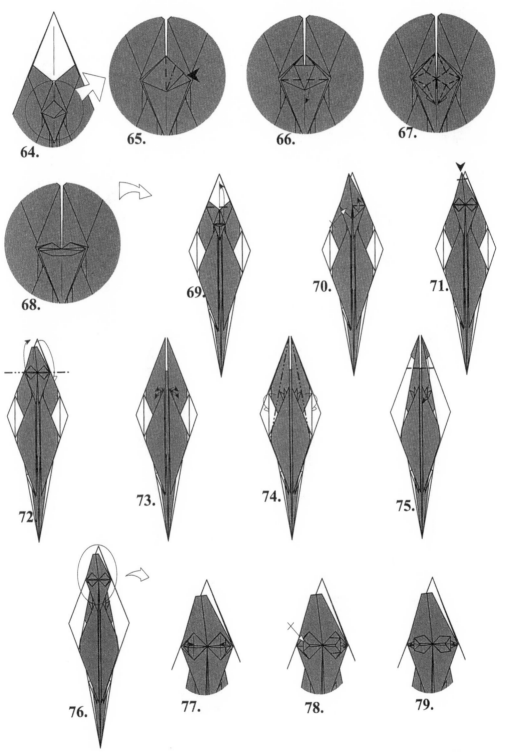

64.

65.

66.

67.

68.

69.

70.

71.

72

73.

74.

75.

76.

77.

78.

79.

113

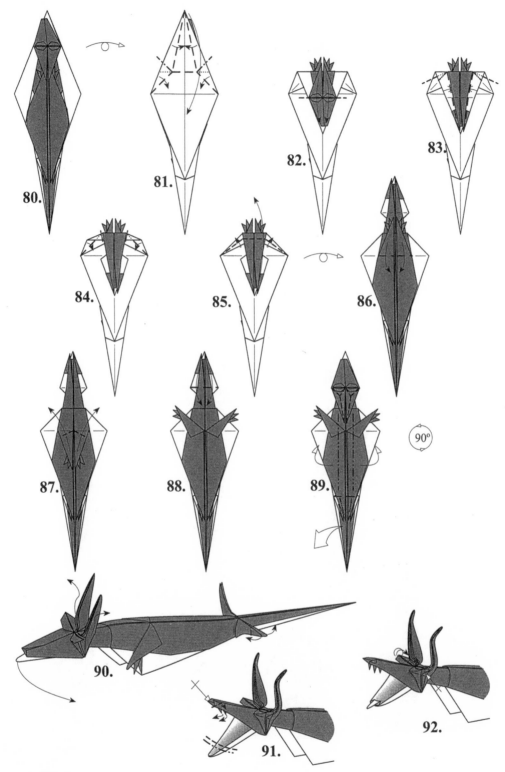

80.

81.

82.

83.

84.

85.

86.

87.

88.

89.

90°

90.

91.

92.

114

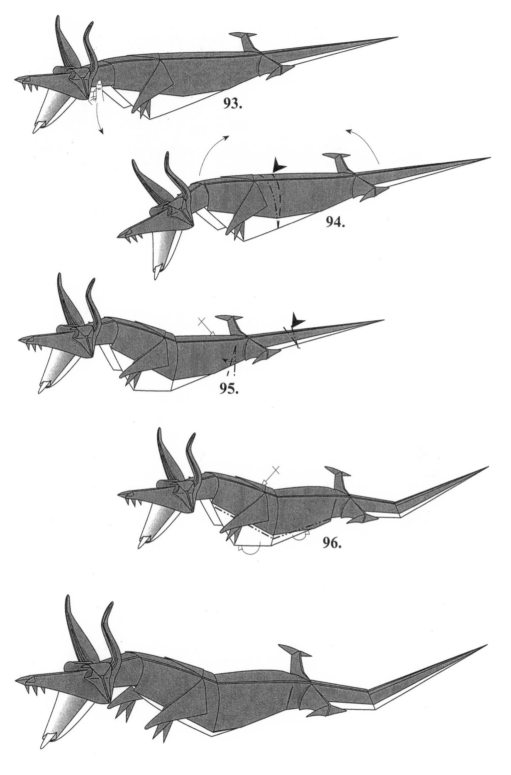

93.

94.

95.

96.

Three-Headed Dragon

This is a giant, fire-breathing, fabled reptile, which is covered with scales, looks terrible, and has poisonous breath.

Author: J. Aníbal Voyer Iniesta

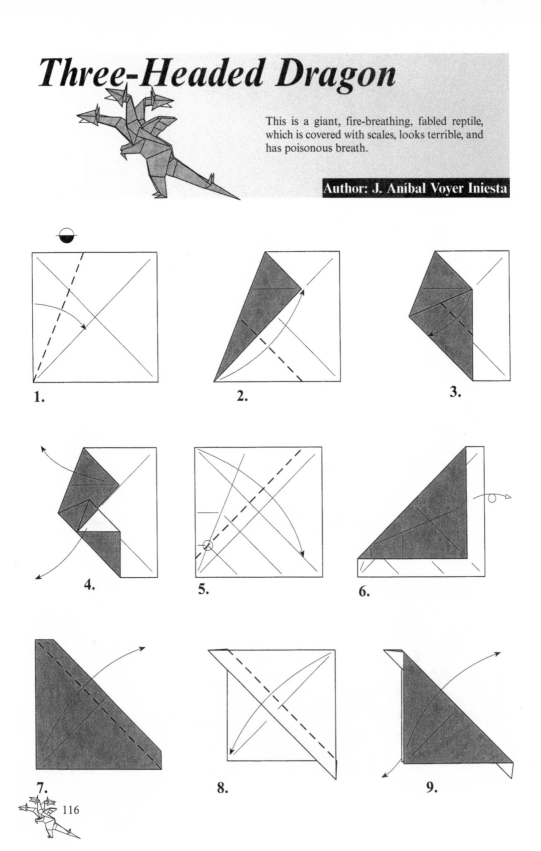

1.

2.

3.

4.

5.

6.

7.

8.

9.

116

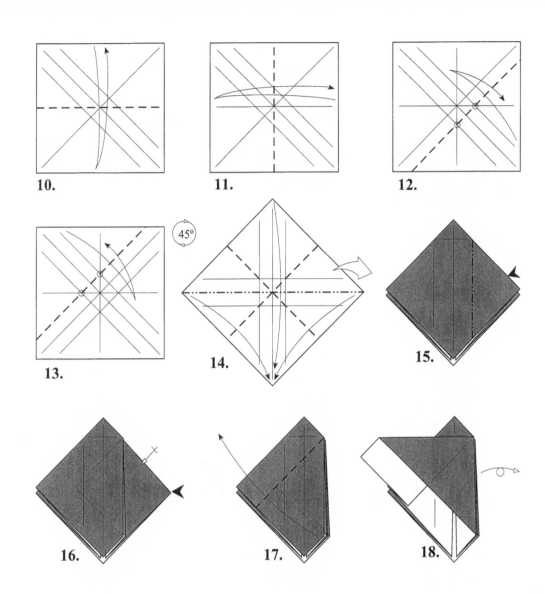

10.

11.

12.

45°

13.

14.

15.

16.

17.

18.

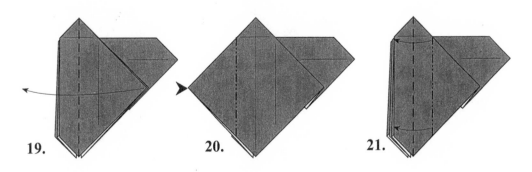

19.

20.

21.

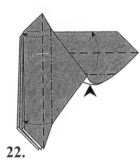

22.

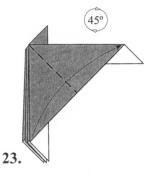

45°

23.

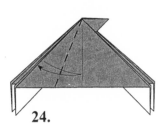

24.

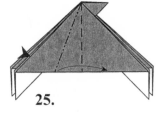

25.

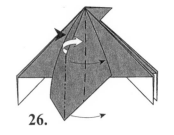

26.

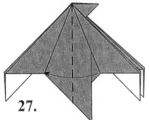

27.

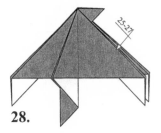

28.

25-27

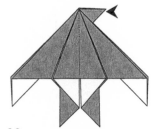

29. Leave two flaps on either side.

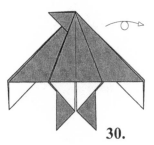

30.

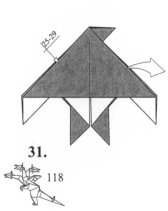

25-29

31.

118

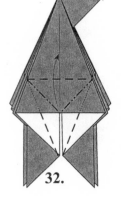

32.

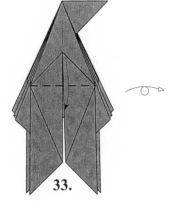

33.

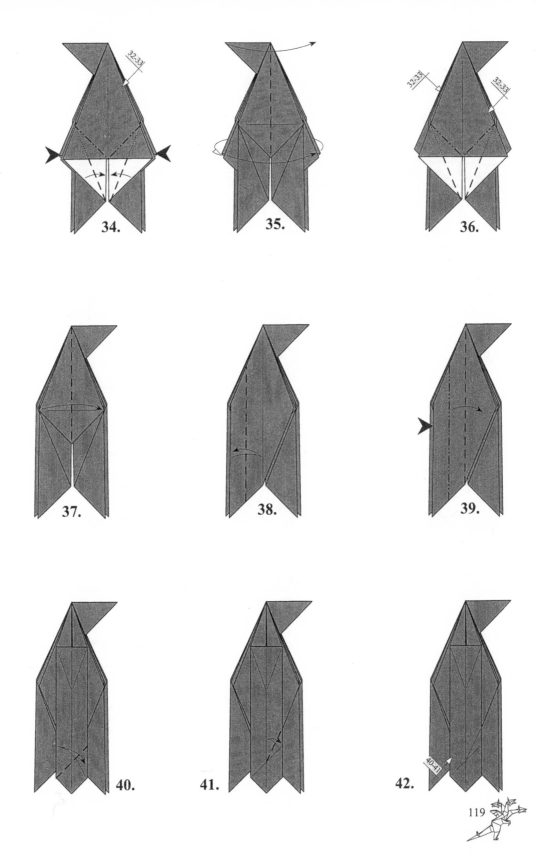

34.

35.

36.

37.

38.

39.

40.

41.

42.

119

43.

44.

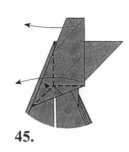

45.

46.

47.

48.

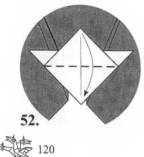

49. Turn the corner inside-out.

50.

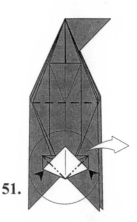

51.

52.

53.

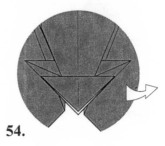

54.

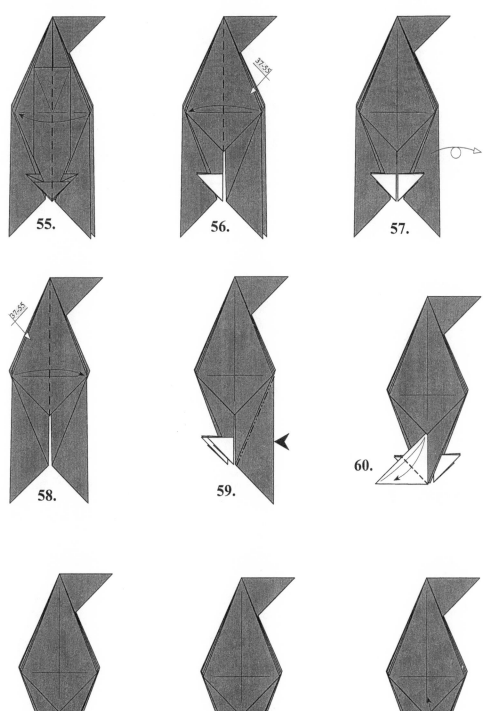

55.

56.

37-55

57.

37-55

58.

59.

60.

61.

62.

63.

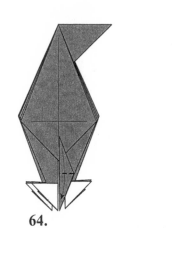

64.

65. Leave two flaps on either side.

66.

67.

68.

69.

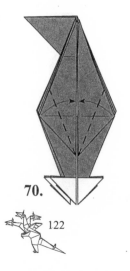

70.

71.

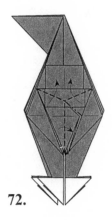

72.

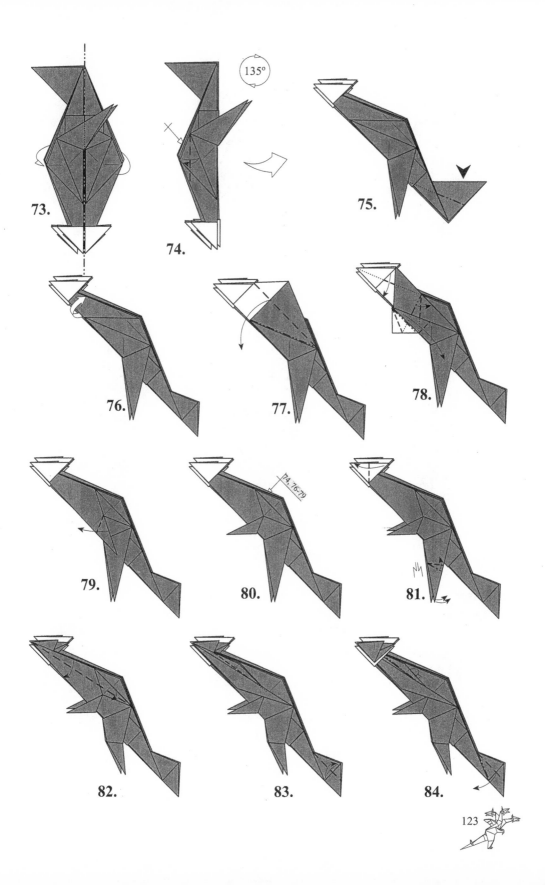

73.

74.

135°

75.

76.

77.

78.

79.

80.

74, 76-79

81.

82.

83.

84.

123

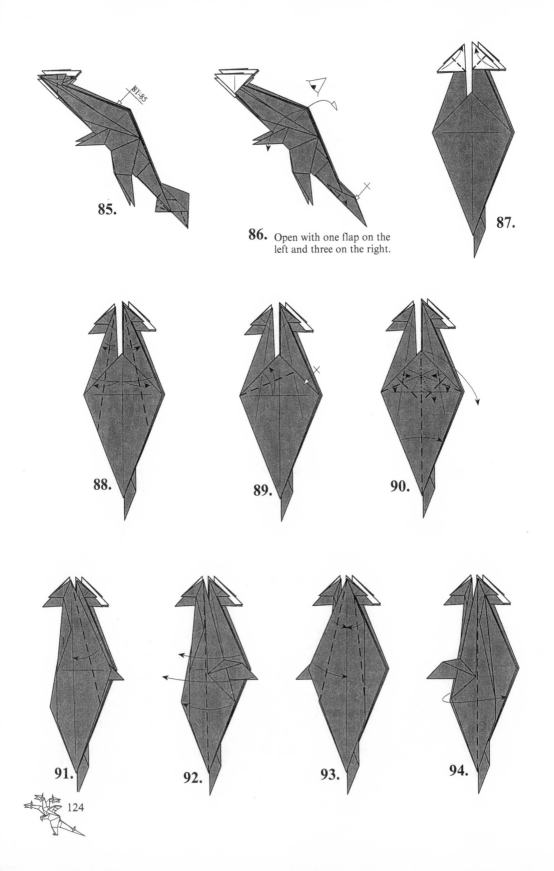

85.

86. Open with one flap on the left and three on the right.

87.

88.

89.

90.

91.

92.

93.

94.

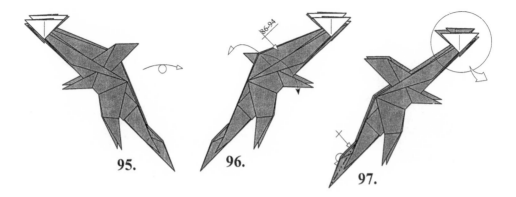

95.

96.

97.

 **98.**

99.

100.

101.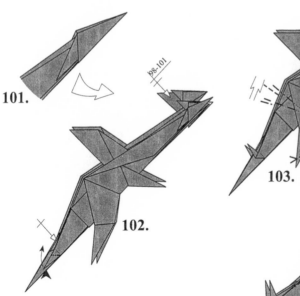

102.

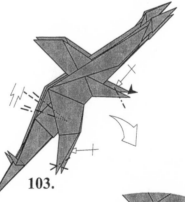

103.

104.

105.

106.

107.

108.

109.

110.

111.

112.

126

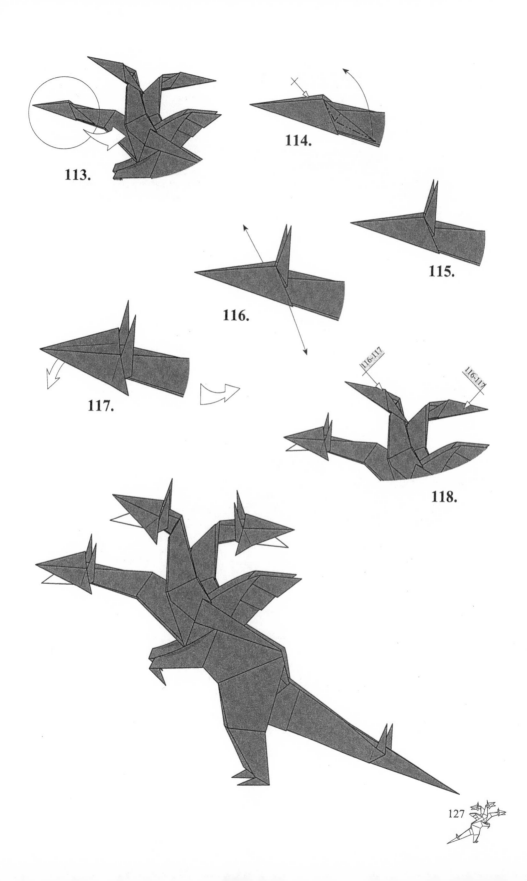

113.

114.

115.

116.

117.

118.

116-117

116-117

Dragon with Warrior

Although dragons are antisocial beings who do not enjoy the company of humans, sometimes they can make temporary pacts with them to acquire an end. This includes allowing humans to ride them.

Author: J. Aníbal Voyer Iniesta

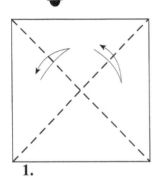

1.

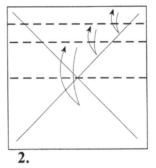

2.

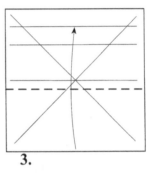

3.

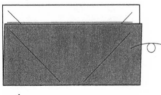

4.

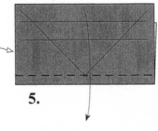

5.

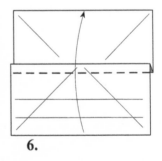

6.

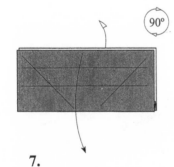

7.

90°

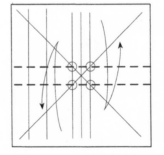

8.

9.

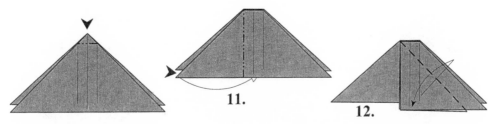

10.

11.

12.

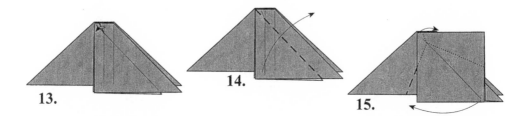

13.

14.

15.

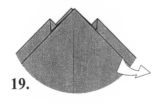

16.

11-15

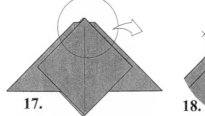

17.

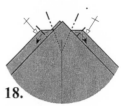

18.

19.

20.

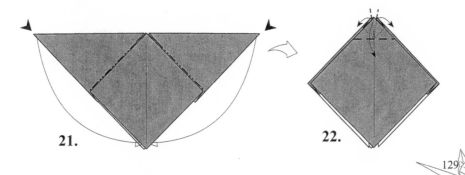

21.

22.

129

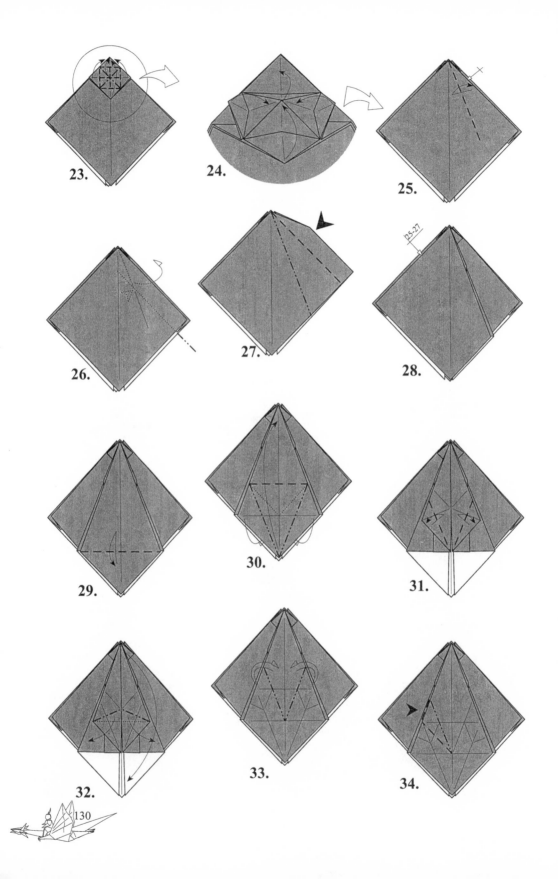

23.

24.

25.

26.

27.

28.

29.

30.

31.

32.

33.

34.

25-27

130

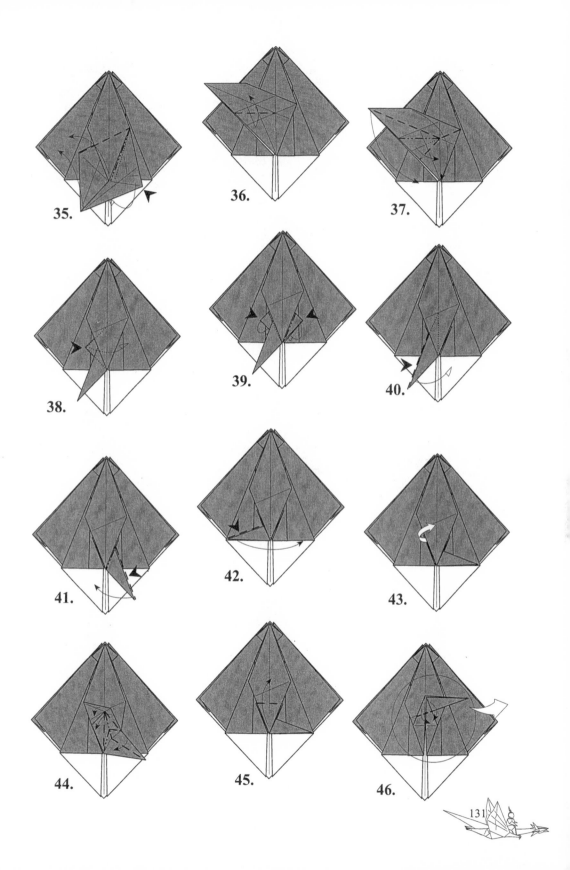

35.

36.

37.

38.

39.

40.

41.

42.

43.

44.

45.

46.

131

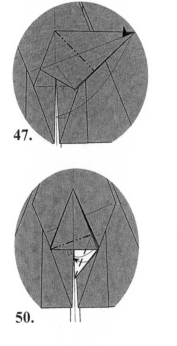

47.

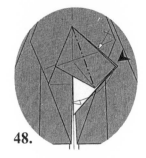

48.

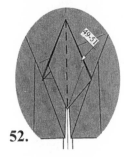

49.

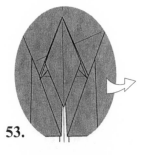

50.

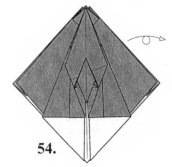

51.

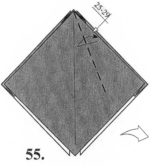

52.

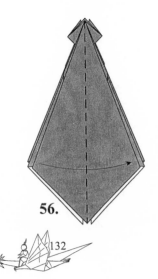

53.

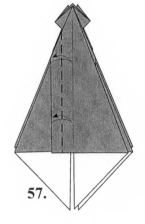

54.

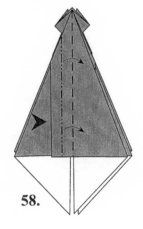

55.

56.

57.

58.

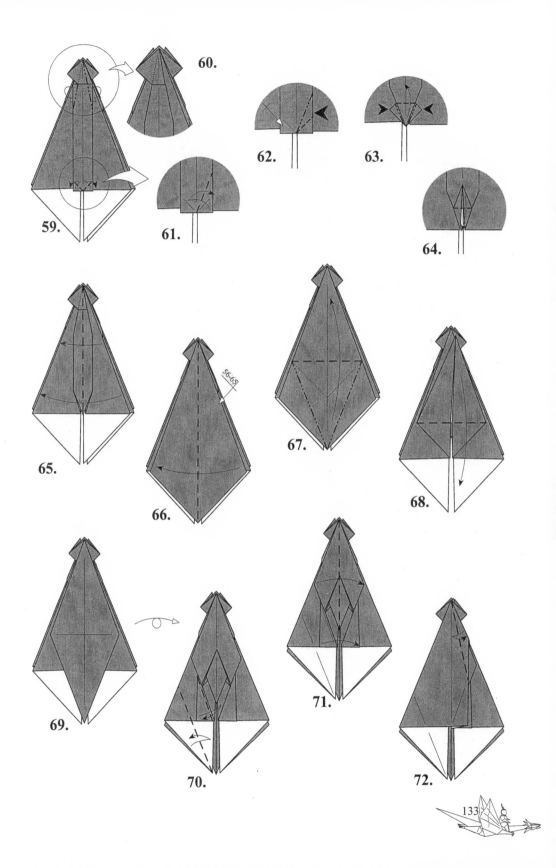

59.

60.

61.

62.

63.

64.

65.

66.

67.

68.

69.

70.

71.

72.

133

73.

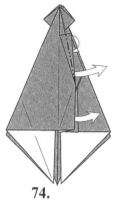

74.

75. This is 3D.

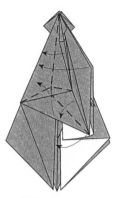

76. This is 3D.

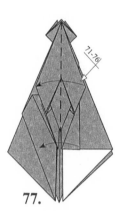

77.

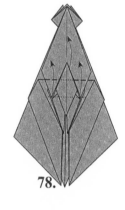

78.

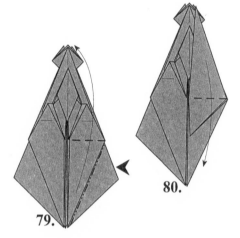

79.

80.

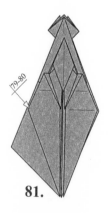

81.

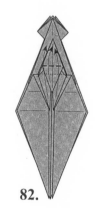

82.

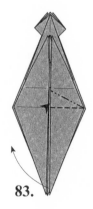

83.

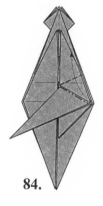

84.

134

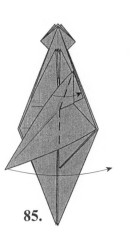

85.

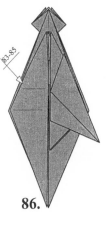

86.

83-85

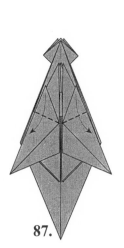

87.

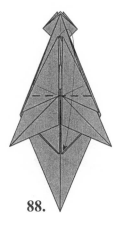

88.

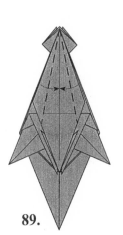

89.

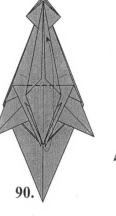

90.

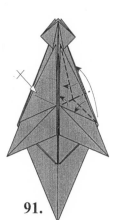

91.

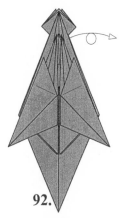

92.

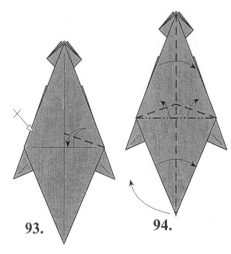

93.

94.

95.

96.

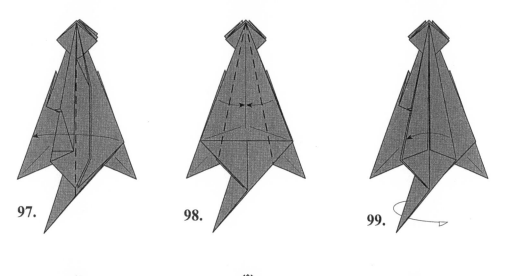

97.

98.

99.

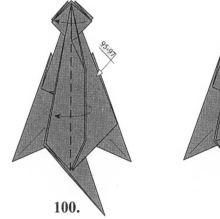

100.

95-97

101.

102. Fold without creasing.

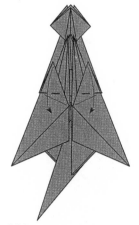

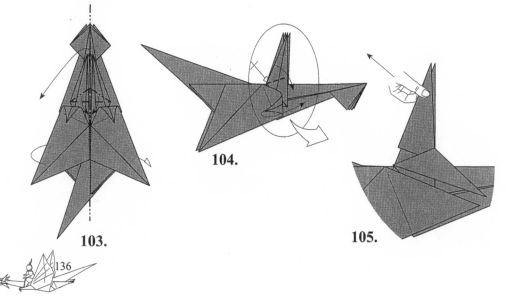

103.

104.

105.

136

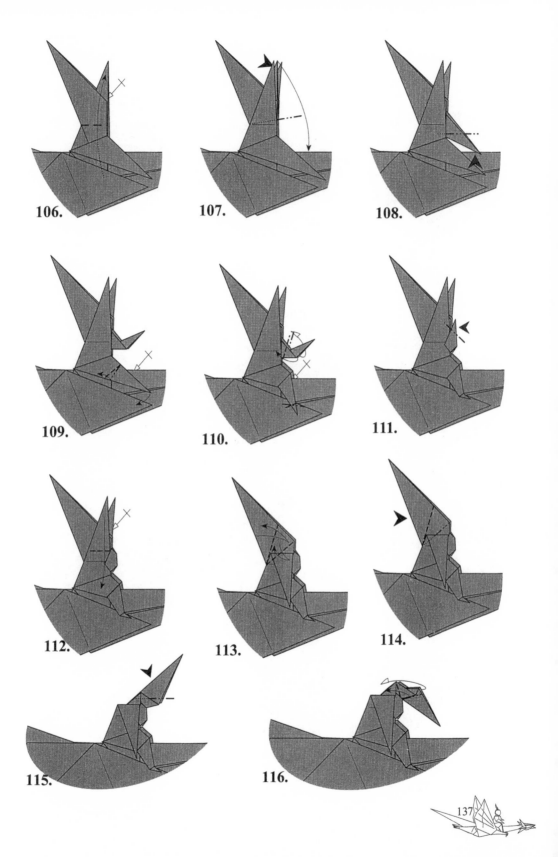

106.

107.

108.

109.

110.

111.

112.

113.

114.

115.

116.

137

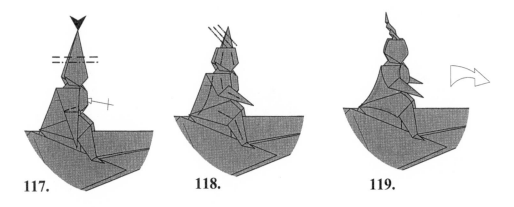

117. **118.** **119.**

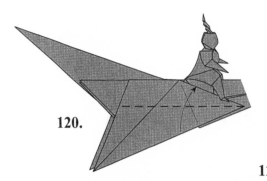

120.

121.

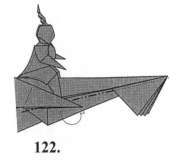

122.

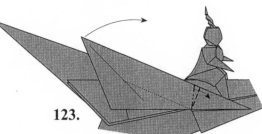

123.

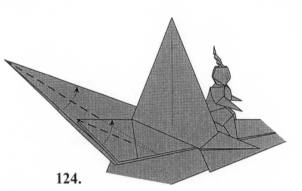

124.

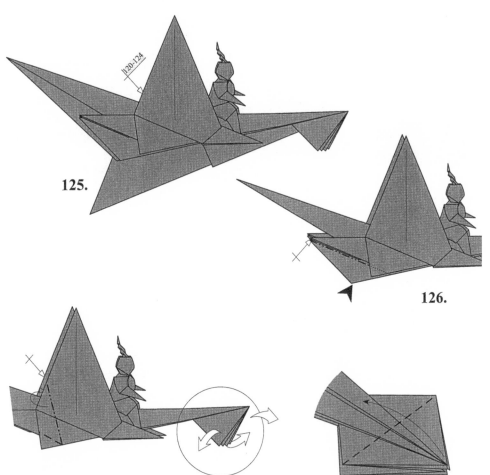

125.

120–124

126.

127.

128.

129.

130.

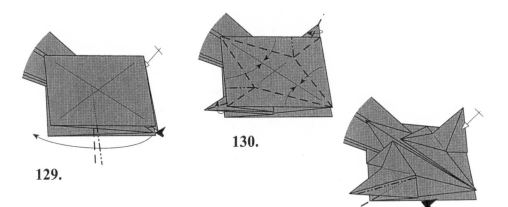

131.

139

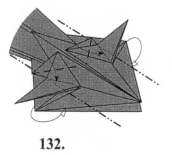

132.

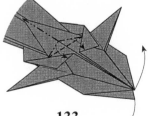

133.

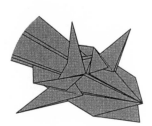

134.

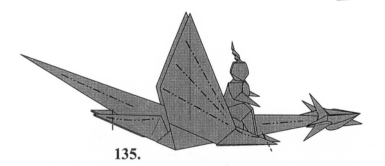

135.

Dragon with Wizard

Taming a dragon and using it as a mount is one way to prove that one has achieved the highest level of wizardry. This enslaving of the dragon can only be sustained for brief periods and usually ends in the death of the wizard.

Author: J. Aníbal Voyer Iniesta

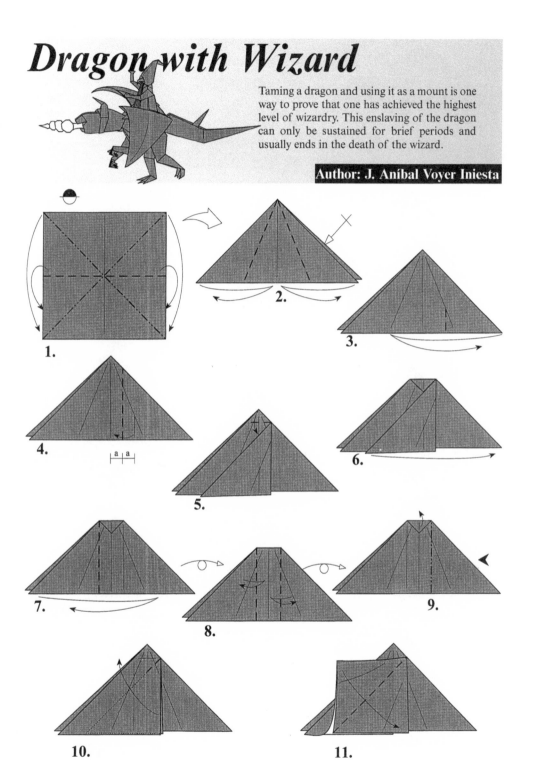

1.

2.

3.

4.

5.

6.

7.

8.

9.

10.

11.

141

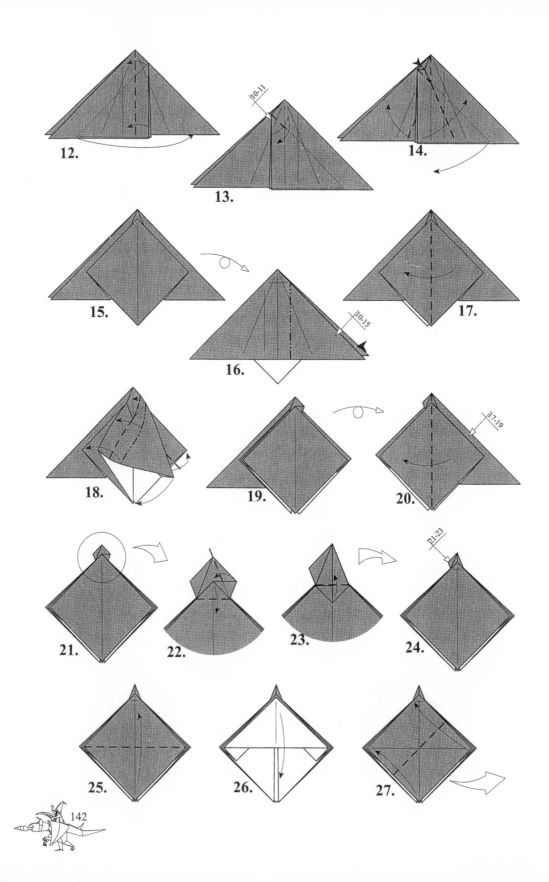

12.

13.

14.

15.

16.

17.

18.

19.

20.

21.

22.

23.

24.

25.

26.

27.

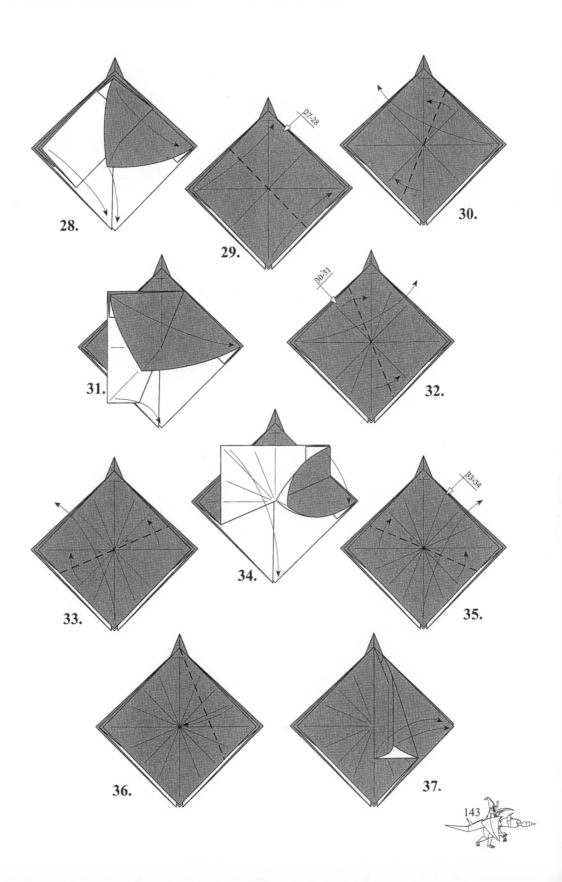

28.

29. 27-28

30.

31.

32. 30-31

33.

34.

35. 33-34

36.

37.

143

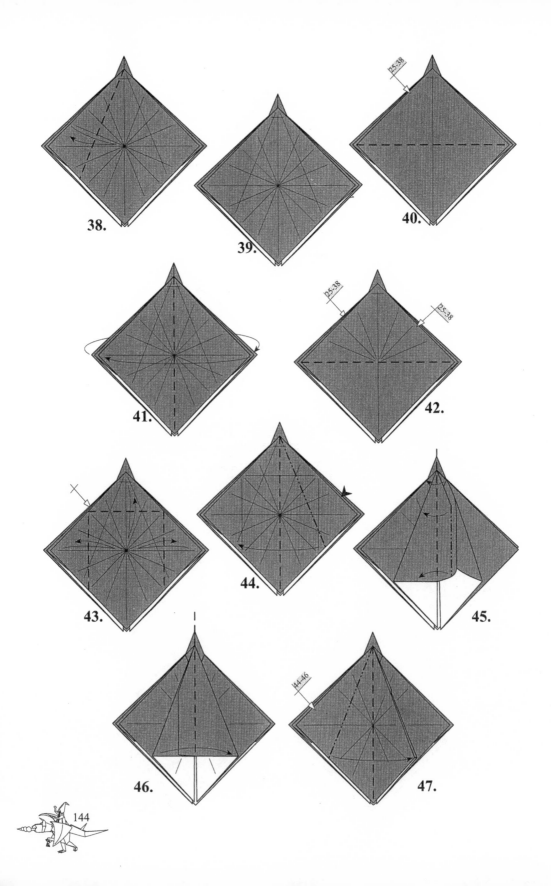

38.

39.

40.

41.

42.

43.

44.

45.

46.

47.

144

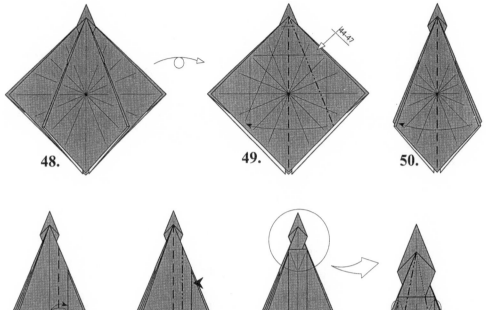

48.

49.

50.

51.

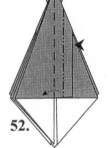

52.

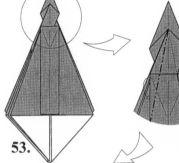

53.

54.

55.

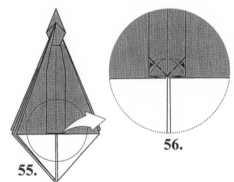

56.

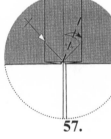

57.

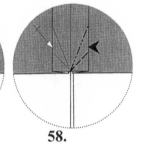

58.

59.

60.

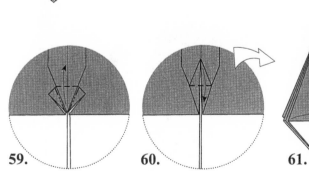

61.

62.

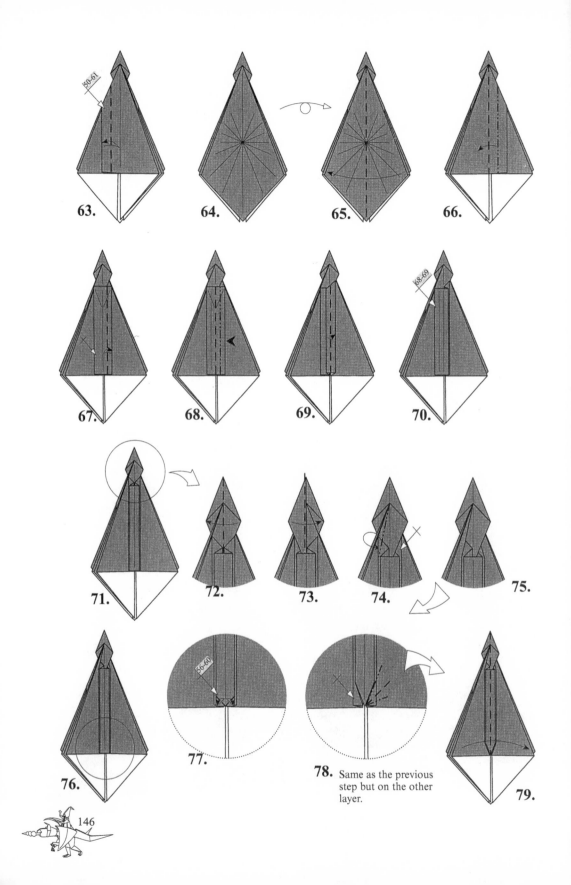

63.

64.

65.

66.

67.

68.

69.

70.

71.

72.

73.

74.

75.

76.

77.

78. Same as the previous step but on the other layer.

79.

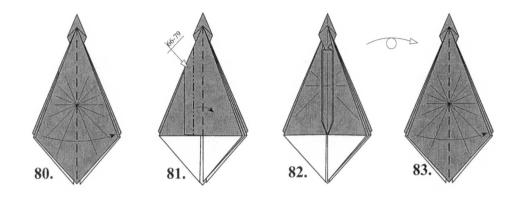

80.

81.

82.

83.

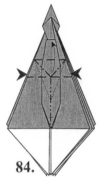

84.

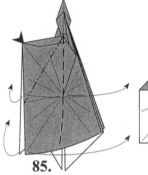

85.

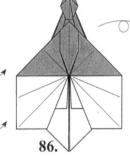

86.

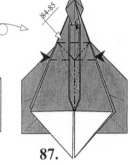

87.

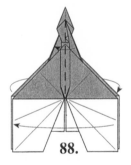

88.

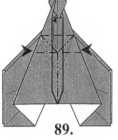

89.

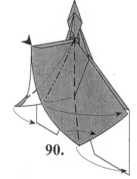

90.

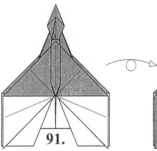

91.

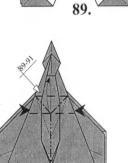

92.

93. Only fold the first layer for each arrow.

147

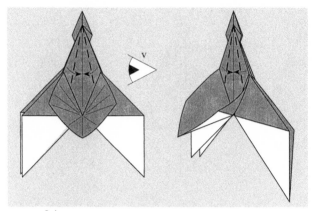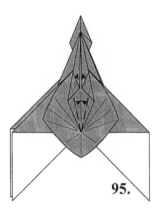

95.

94. Both figures are of the same step.
The second is seen from point v.

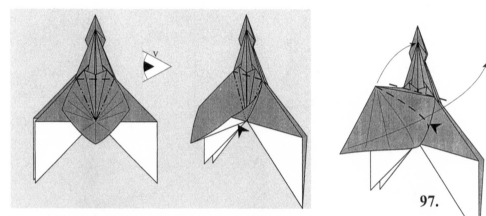

97.

96. Both figures are of the same step.
The second is seen from point v.

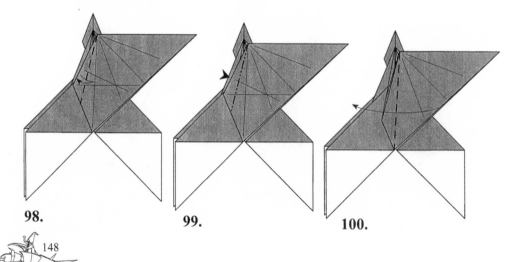

98.

99.

100.

148

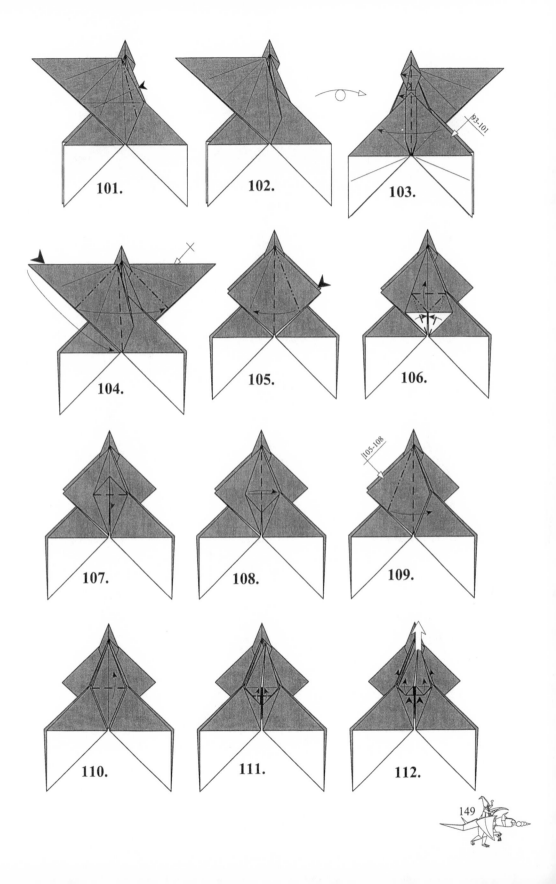

101.

102.

103.

93-101

104.

105.

106.

107.

108.

109.

105-108

110.

111.

112.

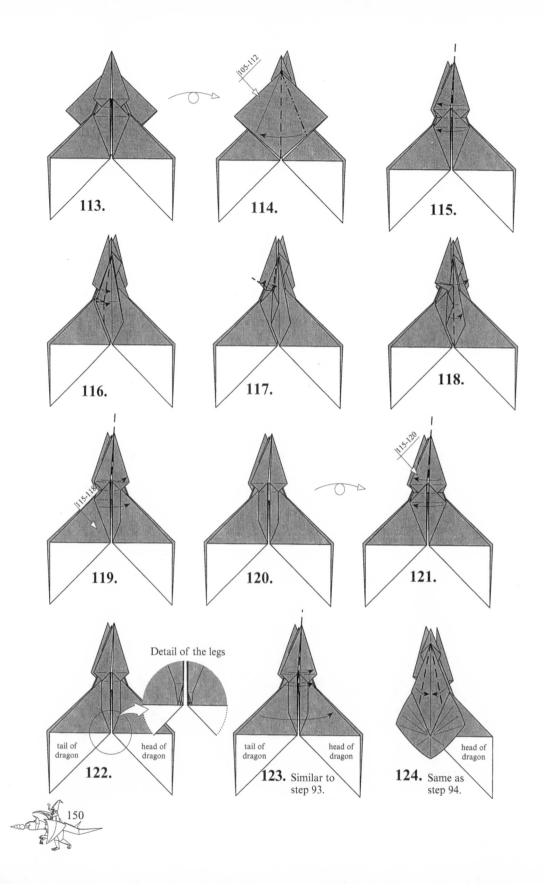

113.

105-112

114.

115.

116.

117.

118.

115-118

119.

120.

115-120

121.

Detail of the legs

tail of dragon
head of dragon

122.

tail of dragon
head of dragon

123. Similar to step 93.

head of dragon

124. Same as step 94.

150

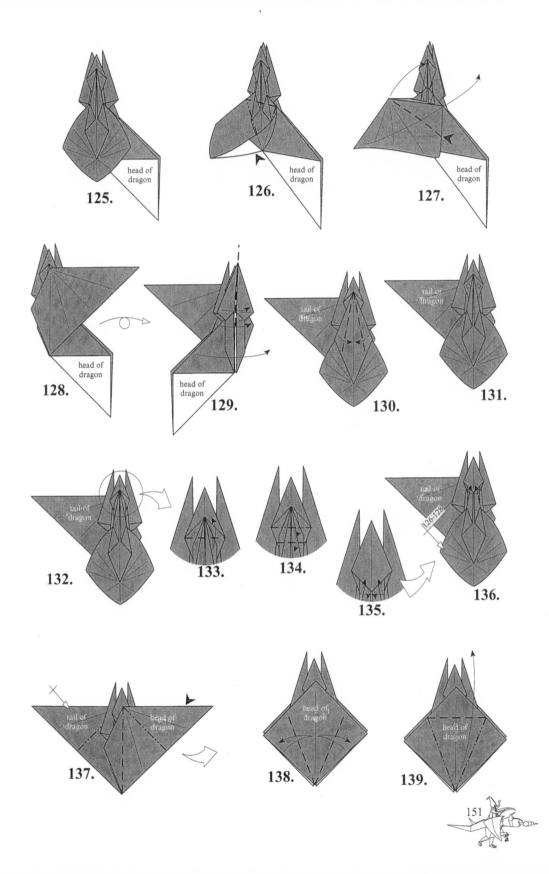

125. head of
dragon

126. head of
dragon

127. head of
dragon

128. head of
dragon

129. head of
dragon

130. tail of
dragon

131. tail of
dragon

132. tail of
dragon

133.

134.

135.

136. tail of
dragon · 126-128

137. tail of
dragon · head of
dragon

138. head of
dragon

139. head of
dragon

151

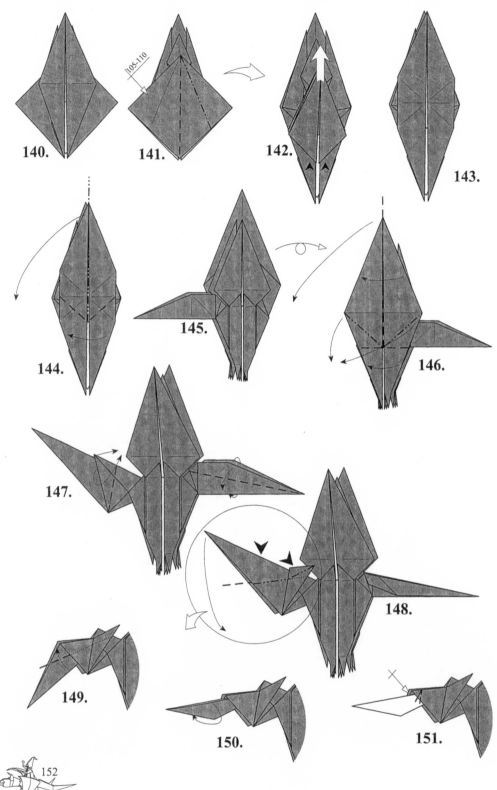

140.

141.   105-110

142.

143.

144.

145.

146.

147.

148.

149.

150.

151.

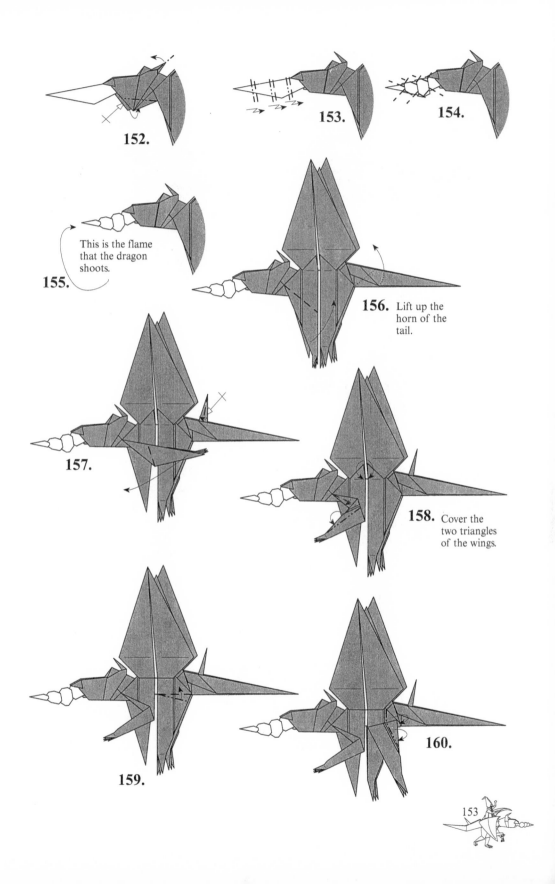

152.

153.

154.

155. This is the flame that the dragon shoots.

156. Lift up the horn of the tail.

157.

158. Cover the two triangles of the wings.

159.

160.

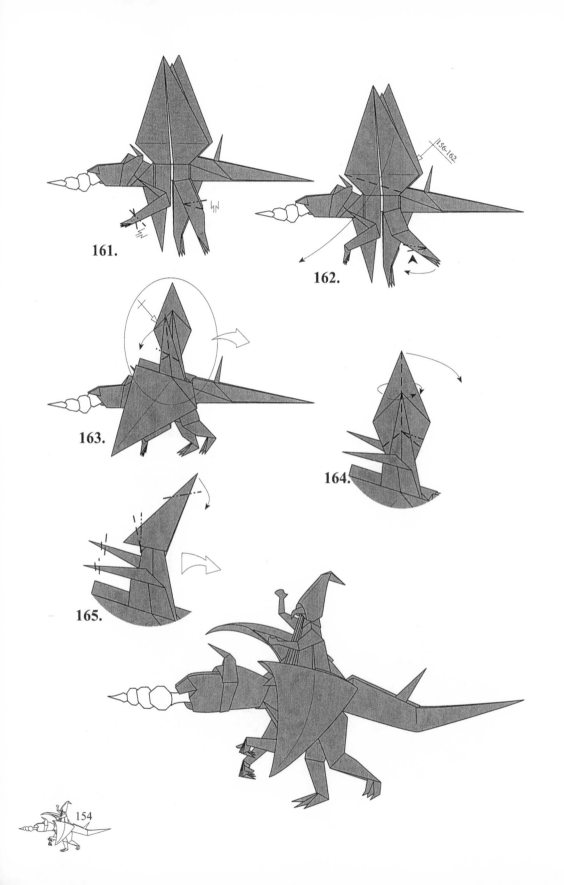

161.

162.

163.

164.

165.

Witch

This is a woman who, according to folklore, has a pact with the devil and can make extraordinary things happen on his behalf.

Author: J. Aníbal Voyer Iniesta

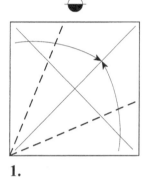

1.

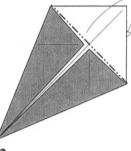

2.

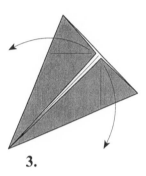

3.

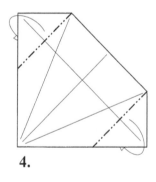

4.

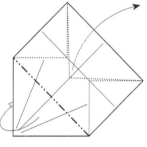

5.

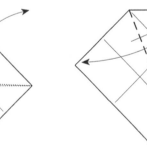

6.

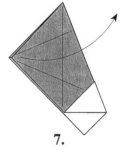

7.

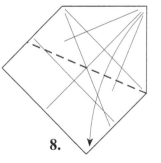

8.

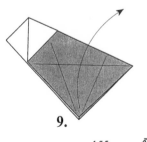

9.

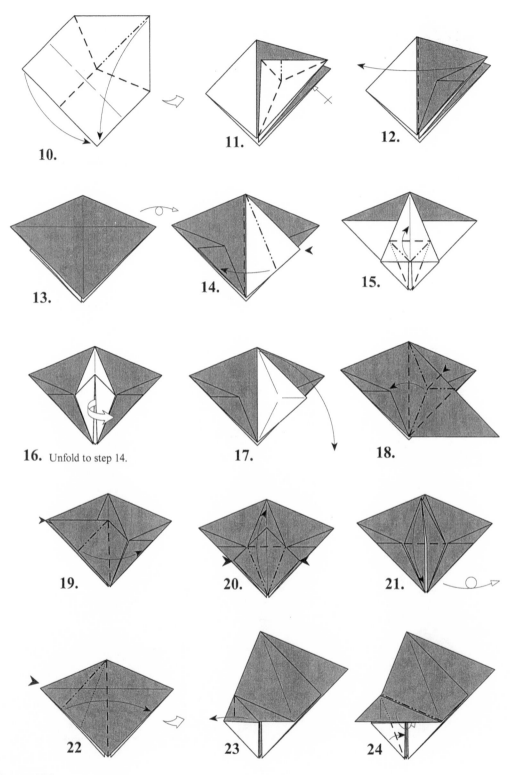

10.

11.

12.

13.

14.

15.

16. Unfold to step 14.

17.

18.

19.

20.

21.

22.

23.

24.

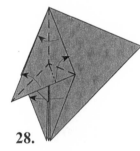
25.

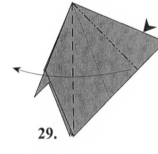
26.

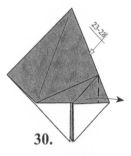
27.

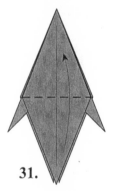
28.

29.

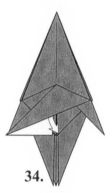
30.

31.

32.

33.

34.

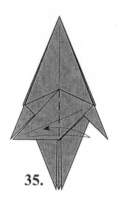
35.

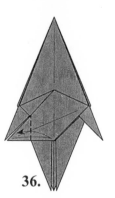
36.

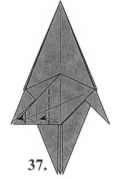
37.

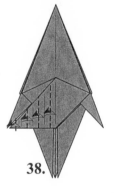
38.

157

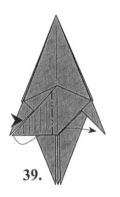

39.

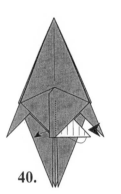

40.

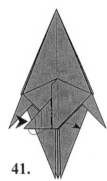

41.

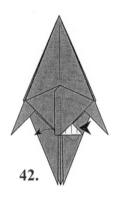

42.

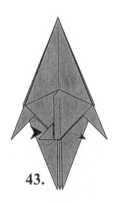

43.

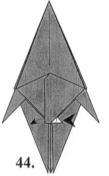

44.

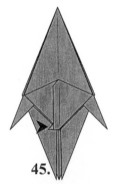

45.

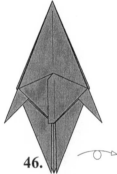

46.

47.

48.

49.

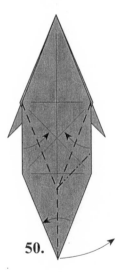

50.

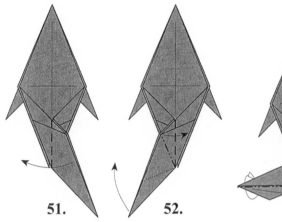

51.

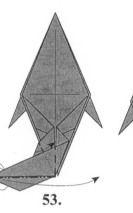

52.

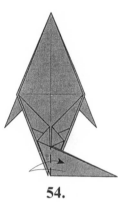

53.

54.

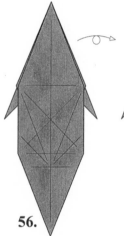

55.

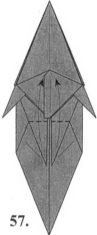

56.

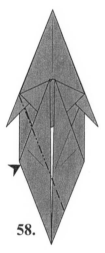

57.

58.

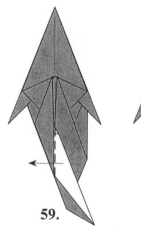

59.

60.

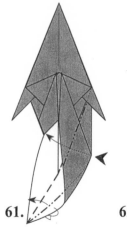

61.

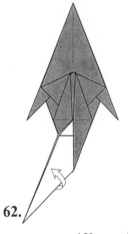

62.

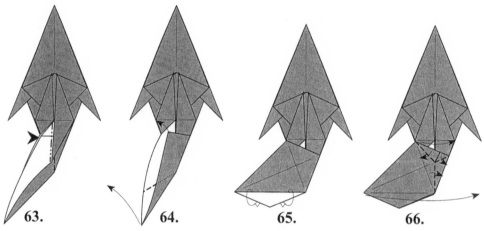

63. **64.** **65.** **66.**

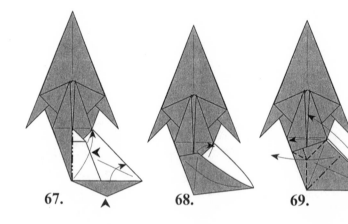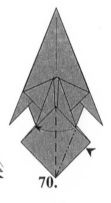

67. **68.** **69.** **70.**

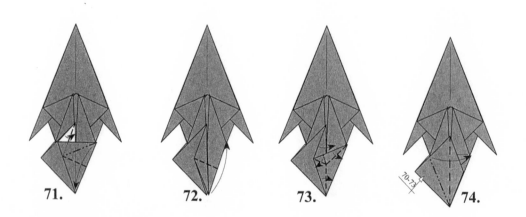

71. **72.** **73.** **74.**

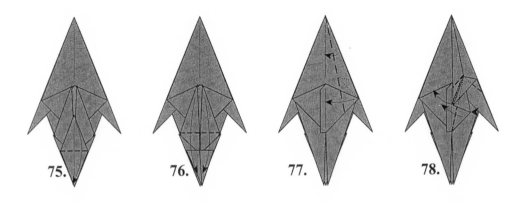

75.

76.

77.

78.

79.

80.

81.

82.

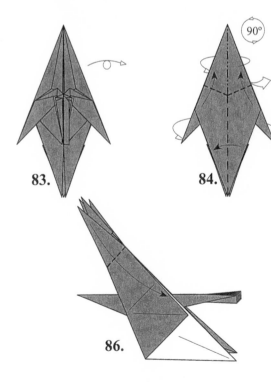

83.

84.

90°

85.

86.

87.

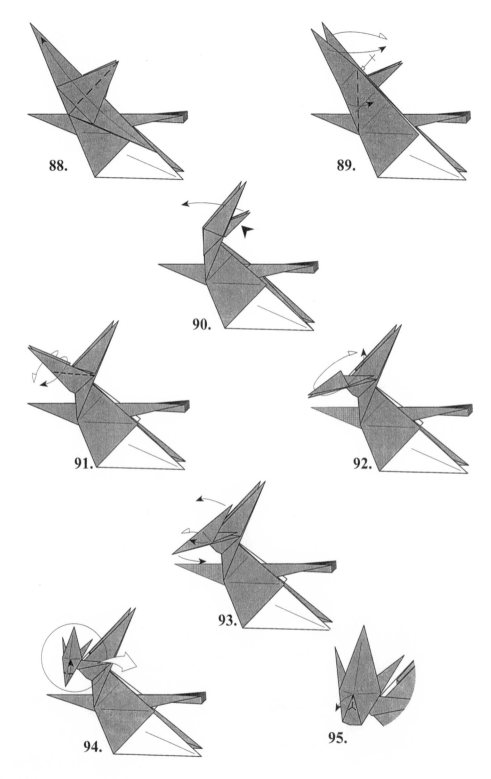

88.

89.

90.

91.

92.

93.

94.

95.

96.

97.

98.

99.

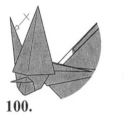

100.

101.

102.

103.

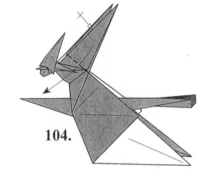

104.

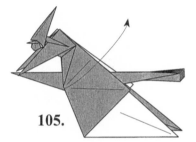

105.

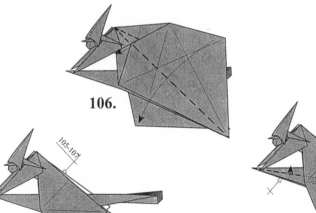

106.

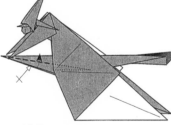

107.

108. Fold two layers together and repeat behind.

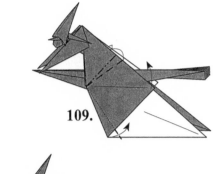

109.

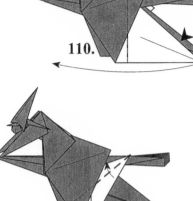

110.

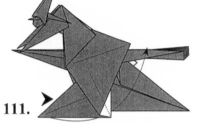

111.

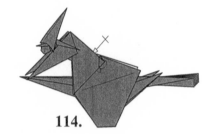

112.

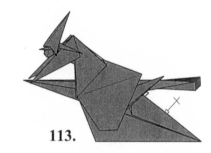

113.

114.

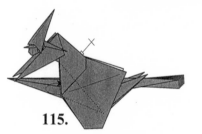

115.

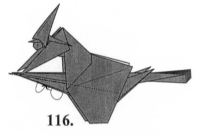

116.

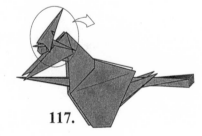

117.

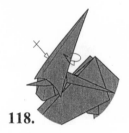

118.

119.

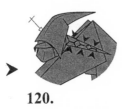

120.

121.

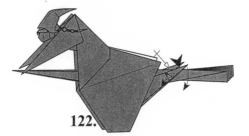

122.

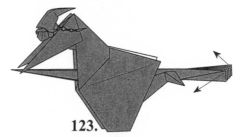

123.

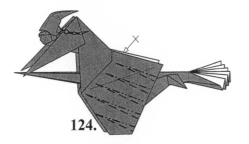

124.

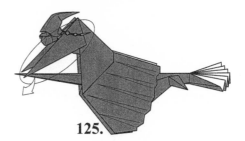

125.

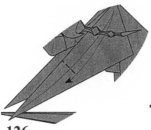

126.

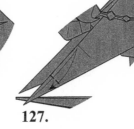

127.

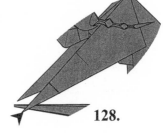

128.

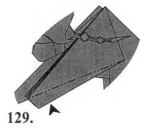

129.

130.

131.

165

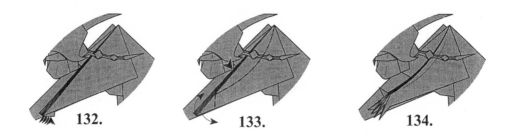

132. **133.** **134.**

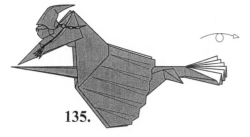

135.

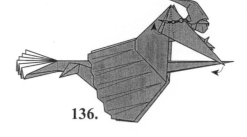

136.

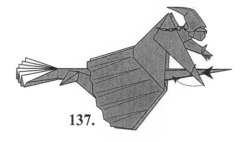

137.

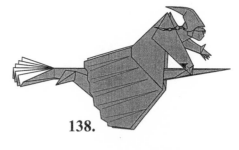

138.

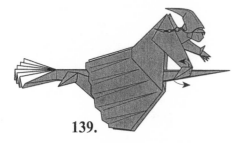

139.

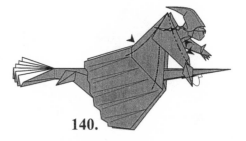

140.

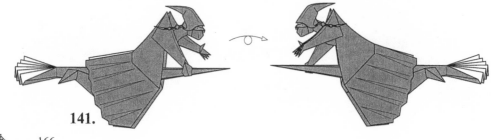

141.

Wasp

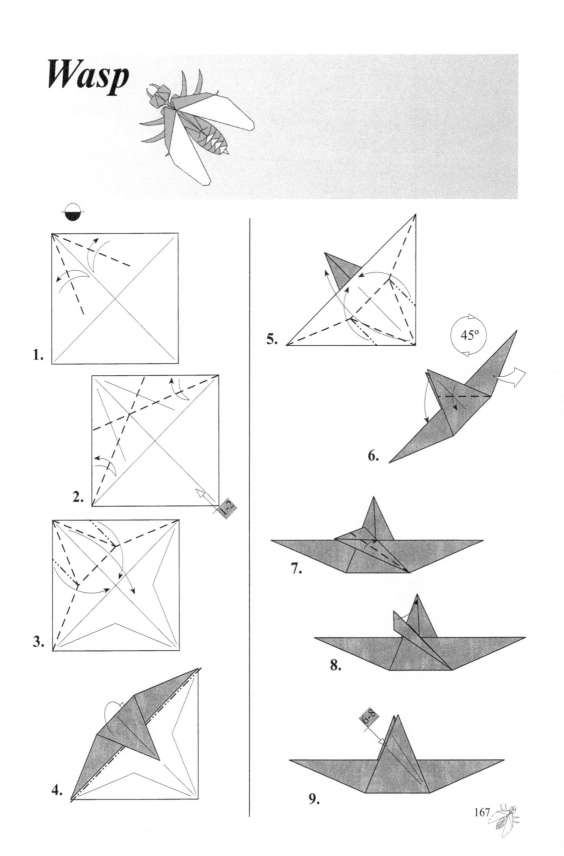

1.

2.

3.

4.

5.

6.

45°

7.

8.

9.

167

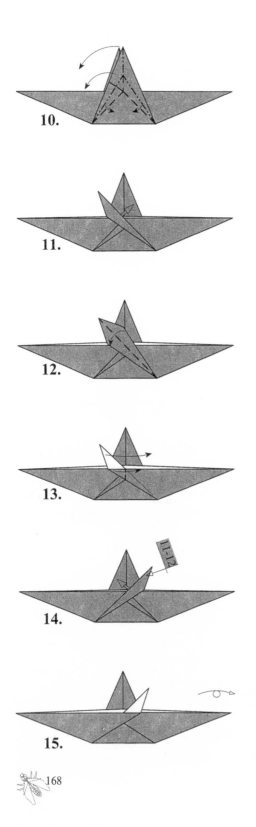

10.

11.

12.

13.

14.

15.

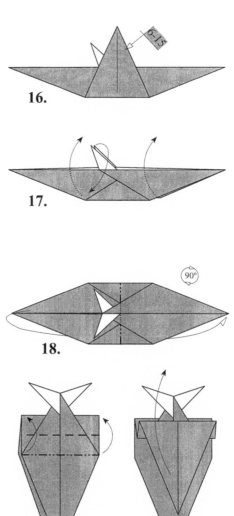

16.

17.

18.

19.

20.

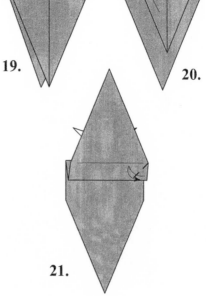

21.

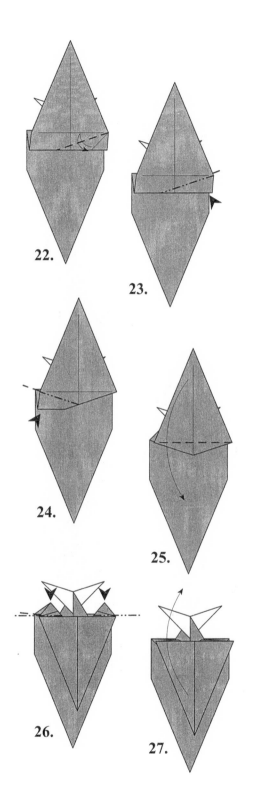

22.

23.

24.

25.

26.

27.

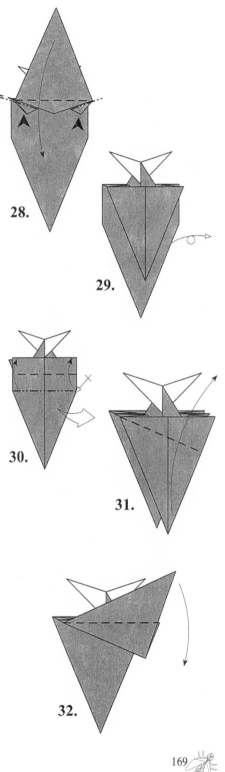

28.

29.

30.

31.

32.

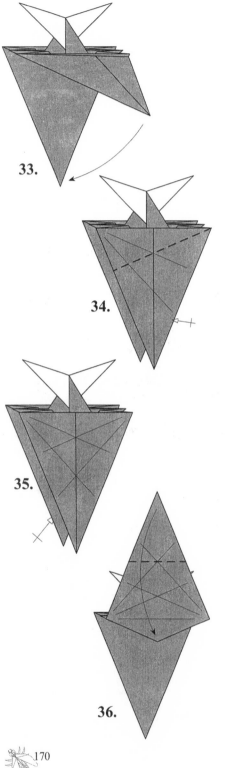

33.

34.

35.

36.

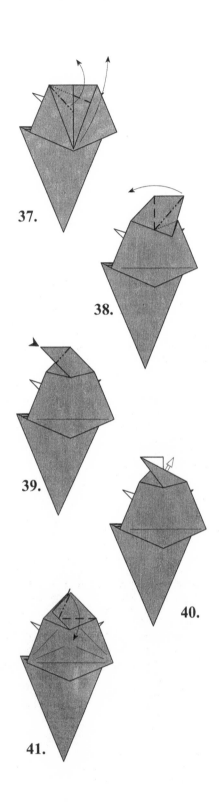

37.

38.

39.

40.

41.

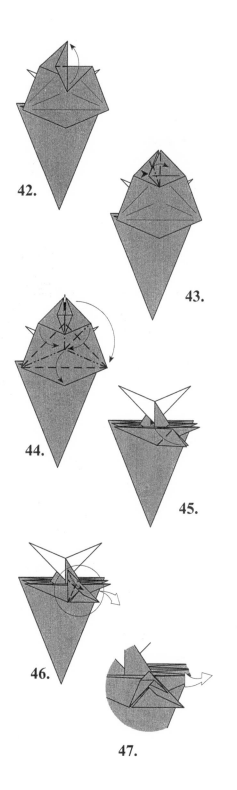

42.

43.

44.

45.

46.

47.

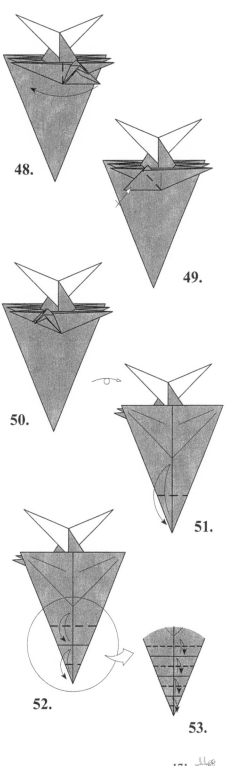

48.

49.

50.

51.

52.

53.

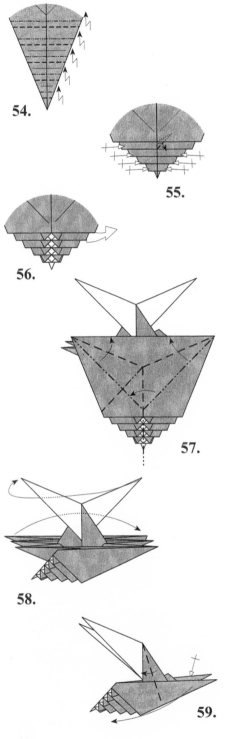

54.

55.

56.

57.

58.

59.

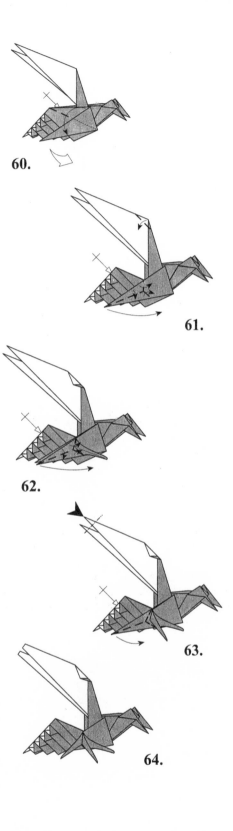

60.

61.

62.

63.

64.

65.

66.

67.

68.